Destiny is calling on the youth to change the world, but the irony is that the youths are waiting for the elderly to change the world. Yet the elderly know; that only the youth can change the world.

.

—C. H. Zudes—

There is so much to be known,
 Life is Short and Life is not Life without
Knowledge. The excellent truth is acquire
Knowledge from everyone

—Baltasar Gracian—
(1601-1658).

DEDICATION

His Eminence

John Cardinal Onaiyekan

For his Influence in upholding the Truth
Ignored by many and his balanced moral
guide to the Church and her youth.

Especially for his 70th Anniversary

****

Very REV. Fr. Camillus Ejike Mbaka

For refocusing the youth in Spirituality, showing direction
in their moment of Crisis, and also funding the hopeless
to find hope

****

His Excellency

Mr. Peter Obi

For pioneering Moral Stability in the Nation's politics and
pointing direction to Philosophers' roles in generational
transformational leadership

****

His Excellency

Barr. Sullivan Iheanacho Chime

For his Commitment in reshaping the moral life of the
youth in the coal city, especially his courage in putting to
near end the evil of students cultism which he inherited.
Are youth's models that politics can stop existing evil?

ACKNOWLEDGEMENT

I gratefully appreciate Graces and Privileges from the Almighty God. I am most indebted to everyone I have come across in my youthful-eventful life, especially all those I met in times of vicissitudes that characterized life's uncertainties. Those who led me from confusions to directions. I thank you all. To my beloved but late Father Mr. G. U. Ozoude, whose ways remain a model and my late elderly brother Mr. James Chukwu-Emeka Ozoude whose absence has cast many shadows. All the good ancestors and all great young people who are no more, kindly Rest in Perfect Peace Amen.

I acknowledge all whose lives are great inspiration to the young ones. Rt. Hon. Wakil Mohammed (Dearly Honourable Minister of State). Hon. Chief Dubem Onyia (KSJ). I appreciate the leadership splendour of Most Rev. Dr. Callistus Onaga, Our Catholic Bishop of Enugu. Very Rev. Fr. Camillus Ejike Mbaka and Rev. Fr. Paul Ekowa both sponsored my Computer Education in year 2000. Also Rev. Fr. Profs, Emma. Edeh, Obiorah Ike and Chris Anieke. Rev. Fr. Dr. BonaChristus Umeogu (for the Entire Philosophers and its Unizik lecturers) and Prof. Miriam Ikejiani Clark (for their dual foreword to this book). Very Rev. Fr. Ambrose Agu, Very Rev Fr. Uche Obodechina. Very Rev Fr. Theo Anyanwu. Fr. Mike Okoh. Rev. Fr. Chris Amogu all my teachers, Rectors and are friends. All the Priests of Ngwo, I appreciate all friendship of Rev. Frs. Joe

Ozofor, Rev. Fr. Paul and Patrick Ogbozor, Rev. Frs. Evans & Eugene Offor, Rev. Fr. Eugene Ezeofor and Rev. Frs. Cyril and Cletus Eze and Frs. Leo Ukwuani and Leo Ozougwu. Rev Fr. Emma Okwor, Rev. Fr. Matthew Nebo and Good parishioners of St. Joseph's Parish, and entire Priests and Religious of Ngwo Clan. My thanks goes to Very Rev. Fr. John Nwafor and Fr. Mario Egeolu and Fr. Dibia for being ever friendly with the young.

Hon. Dr. Emmanuel Ngwu, Prince Uche and Patrick Ayalogu (the entire staff and management of Phinomar Nigeria Ltd) and all who supported me. I also acknowledge the prominent place of all members of Ngwo Progressive Union Abuja, ably led by Engr. Ikechuwu G. Ozoude and the influences of other great people like Mr. Anthony Ani, Engr. Dom. Onoh, and Chief Linus Ozoagu, and all of you! I appreciate Dr. Okey Orji, Sir Chris Onoh, Mr Chris Ukwuani and Mr. Nduka Ozougwu and friends too special for mention like Mr. Raphael Ozoude and Mr. Ikenna Eze of NBL all Ngwo people in Lagos & everywhere.

The vibrant people of Holy Cross Parish Gwarinpa Abuja, benevolently led by Very Rev. Fr. Chris Bologo and ably assisted by Rev. Fr. Alex Ogbanufe. The entire Members of St. Peter Igbo Cath. Community magnanimously led by Prince Obinna Okwuaka (KSM) and Engr. Linus Ugwa.

Also the influences of Chief Dr. M.A.N. Ejiofor, Chief N. I Awaji, Mr. Silver Ikowete and Barr. Chike Thomson Chukwurah. Dr. A. Ikenga-Metuh and Mr. Ken Chime endured my weaknesses, especially Mr. Mike Obasi and Chief Anthony Nwachukwu.

Also acknowledged are prominent feminine roles of Mrs. Adaku Odom, who always deserve special mention as she set my literary success in motion. Mrs. Ngozi Mbaka and Mrs. Rose Okonkwo, Mrs. Nkechi Ebinaso and Princess Chinelo Onwudiwe on behalf of all our great mothers of the Holy Cross. Everyone I met in Holy Cross, have helped me to stand better today, especially Mrs. Buella Chukwumah and Mr. Arthur and Mrs. Felicia Osuji families.

I acknowledge my family members; my mother Mrs. Ijeoma C. Ozoude. My brothers, Mr. Benedict and Mr. Benjamin and Amaka-Grace, Amuche and Onyeka, Mrs. Nneka and Mrs. Ada and Mrs. Concilia Ozoude. I appreciate Lady Ann Ebere Uzoamaka Ude, for all she is to me and my Cousins Uche, Anayo, Ozoude entire relations for all Ngwo Youths . Engr. Iyke Onoh (Icon and al our friends, of Ngwo Unizik team). Mr. Emmanuel Onoh. Mr. Ude Bartholomew Ebuka, Mrs. Chinyere Oyekezie and Lady Blessing Nwatu for all their roles and Mr John Martins and Mrs. Cynthia Eze in whose home in Minna this book was finally completed. My unique friends: Mr. Ifeanyi and Mrs. Peace Chikwelu, Dr. Theo

Nwokocha and Mr. Pat & Mrs. Lovester Ihuoma for their positive influences of friendly attention.

I acknowledge the trendy representative roles of National Youth Council of Nigeria on behalf of the less assisted youths of our continent and Generation. I invite the Youths of our time to collaborate further and closer to generate solutions to the needs and challenges of this generation. Friends and past leaders of the Gwarinpa youth like Mr. Alex, Engr. Uzor Nwachukwu and family, Mr. Ifechi and Mrs. Nk. Dikebuaso, and Mr. Joseph and Ify Anekwe. Mr. Mascot Ohanu and Mr. Emmanuel Ocheni accept my best wishes, and every one of the youths especially those who inspired their fellow youths positively, among who are Mr. John Umennadi, Pharm. Chidi Duru (Marja). Chima Valentine Chukwunwendu, Chief Emeka Ezelioha, Mr. Sabbastine Eke and Mr. Austin and Mrs. Jenny Iniegbu, Mr. Richie and Mrs. Nneka Oleh and more especially Mr. Uwaoma S. Nnachetam. Mrs. Ngozi Udeze. Mr. Johnbosco Oguguo and Lady Thelma Idem and Barr. Pamela Ezendu. Mr. Chris Okenwa and Mr Levi Chikwelu and Mr. Uche Newton and Pharmacist Chima and Dr Mrs. Chioma Udigwe for their families whose commitment and inputs brought in great success to this book. Barr. Kingsley & Mrs. Nkechi Rosemary Alilionwu, Very Rev. Fr. Octavius Moo and Fr. Joseph AkA, of RECOWA-CERAO Secretariat, their staff; Barr. Tina Ene Abakpa, Nkem Ikeze Onyebuchi and Deborah Shogus.

Also, my gratitude goes to Dr. Obi George Bisong (Co-writing the preface of this work). Am always proud of my Publishers Phantom House Books USA and United Kingdom especially Mr. Jeff Tadpole and Mr. T.N Odu for their in contributions modern publishing techniques.

To Sir. Victor Anoliefo for Abuja Literary Society and Dr. Usman Shehu for Abuja Writers Forum and Mr. Ndubuisi Ani the Chairman and Members Association of Nigerian Authors, Enugu Branch I am always thankful. I appreciate Mr. Matthew Offiah for his roles in Africa.

Chief Anthony Anenih for adding guidance to good leadership to fix my generation. Very Rev. Fr. Willy Ojukwu and Fr. Prof. Boniface Obiekezie. Mr. and Mrs Okey and Ijeoma Onyejiuwa for Housing the Author in moment of great need. Madam Adaora Umeorji Nwaokoye of Zenith Bank plc. Prof. Julius Okojie of NUC and Brigadier Gen. JB Olawumi DG of NYSC. Aunty Mary Uchendu DG of National Women Affairs (For showing creativity in Talent so early in life. Rev. Fr Raph Obichie and Rev. Fr. Dominic Isemen now in Congo. High Chief Peter Ojeme (MD \CEO Don P Group), Senator Ike Ekweremmadu, and Rt. Hon. Emeka Ihedioha

FOREWORD

Zudes' discourse on "Youthhood" A Jubilee Harvest of
life and love for the African Youths of Today" is a very
insightful and prosaic presentation of the dilemma
facing the African youths in today's world.

The implications of dialectics of the process of social
change in Religion, Education and Politics on the
African youths have been articulated in this thought
provoking prose.

Zudes, sober reflections on the dilemma of the African
youths is certainly an anodyne for coping with the
perilous predicaments of today's world of change.

Prof. Miriam Ikejiani Clark.

Former DEAN

FACULTY OF THE SOCIAL SCIENCIES

UNIVERSITY OF NIGERIA NSUKKA. (2002 A.D)

FIRST WORD

Youth? Those special class of human zoological group constantly denied attention by the adult section. But, because these Youth, filled with vitality and vigour, come immediately after the adult human family, they have brought much disorder, much heart ache delinquency, to the human zoological family, at large and to the adult section in particular.

In this great work of poetry and prose, this Youth Zudes, has given the youths the attention denied them ever and again; and because, in this work, this attention is coming from one of the Youth, the work suddenly becomes further great. Why? Because only a youth will know the youth (better).

This polyglot work carved its proximate genus: genus proxima on the hard and high way of "Youth-hood"; a metaphysical concept which goes into the foundations of the essence, he witnesses the quiddities of that early in growth that bestrides the narrow world of being a child and being an adult. The author so much took youth-hood into the foundations talked in such a way that the personality of the Youth becomes a camouflage of the narrow world between growing up and grown up.

This harvest of life, love and light for the African Youth is divided into two parts by the author, Part one commenced with the clarification of terms and expressions and through the Jubilee harvest of life for the

C. H. Zudes

African Youth in watchful eyes of African elders and heroes entered the path way of knowledge and culture.

In that pathway, the work established true freedom for the African youth through religion and character, Education and awareness, politics and control, Economics and self-reliance and development and discipline. He ends this part discussing the undeniable place of Talent in human existence.

He points to discovery and development of talent as assignment for everyone. He insists that every true greatness in humans consists in talent developed.

Part 2: This offers prevailing poetic presentations of the vital relevance of controlled emotion in the life of the young in responding to the idea of love. It is a harvest of love for the Africa youth.

True characteristics of love are presented as opposed to lust. The places of friendship leading to happiness are developed as adventures, which often beget wounds or consolations in the act of love.

Prayer and developing integral spiritual life he assures here are routes to correct errors of youthful proliferation in religion (as youth are clear victims).

The author concludes with five Epilogue sonnet poems further offering a means of arousing the curiosity of the audience and wonderful interest of thorough and careful reading. The proper theme of this book should originally read:

"Youth-hood in Africa, a jubilee harvest of life and love for the African youth of today". It has merely been succinctly presented in a fewer terms.

Very Rev. Fr. DR. Bona-Christus Umeogu.

Head of Department, (02-2005),

Senior Lecturer of Philosophy

Nnamdi Azikiwe University, Awka.

PREFACE

Ozoude presents an apologia of a sort for the African youth whose unhealthy/ unfortunate circumstance of life, he argues, came about by the failure of corrupt and unpatriotic elders, the political class and larger society.

He highlight's the abysmal neglect by these groups of leaders of the human ethics and Divine injunctions on youth development. It is an appreciation of random problem of youth's in Africa.

The author, a youth himself, however, still has the confidence, and hopes that the African youth imbued with an unyielding fighting spirit possesses the will-power to, one day, change this status quo and reposition the continent.

Dr. Obi George Bisong

Rtd Regional Director

National Youth Service Corps

PREFACE II

The author has passionately and critically analyzed the environment of the African youth, with particular reference to Nigeria his beloved motherland. His greatest concern has been that, the youth lack the much needed role-models and enabling environment for their growth and self actualization. He bemoans the fact that many an elder and politician leaves much to be desired. He depicts the youth as victims of unjust structures and political systems.

He however exhorts them not to remain helpless victims of the said structures and systems, but to arise and take their destiny into their own hands, putting in optimum use, their God-given talents.

Chris Ozoude, a youth himself, and from his personal experiences in life, challenges the African youth, to trust in Africa, to trust themselves and to work and hope for a brighter future, since, in being that change they desire, they will easily see Africa change to their delight.

Very Rev. Fr. Octavius Moo
Secretary General
Regional Episcopal Conference of West Africa
(RECOWA-CERAO SECRETARIAT).

TABLE OF CONTENTS

[PART 1]

PART 2   [Talent]

PART 1

ONE | Clarification of Concepts

WHAT IS YOUTH HOOD?

The young Aboki was carrying a hoe and a machete trekking along the street and singing to everyone who found time to listen. His song was a begging song and he rendered; "work ino dey, Ten naira I no get, hungry dey kill me"!

The word youthhood is like a hybrid, which is a cross-pollination of two all-important words. The concept in itself is a qualification of one of the pre-eminent stages in human existence. To both evaluate and explain properly this mode of human classification, one will tend to begin with the idea of youth:

It is an early stage in life. The period between being a child and becoming a fully-grown person, and this is particularly applicable to human beings. It is correlated to the adjective young. This expresses the newness or recent nature of a given thing. It gives credence to what is newly born or begun. This consist ideas of both the animate and inanimate phenomenon, as a young boy or girl, a young tree and a young Elephant. Then another adjective youthful goes to qualify what possesses the qualities of a youth.

What then is Hood? Hood easily refers to a covering of something else. It is like an image conferred on what already exists. It is also to be considered like an embroidery (clothes) worn, which decorates existence in natural pattern. Which can be withdrawn when no longer needed.

Therefore, youthhood is like a (time of) endowment, which comes like a springing star. This is a state of progressive advancement in people's life. It is a prominent stage in the metamorphic development of man. This consists of both masculine and feminine gender in human person, who shares the middle stage of life. Youths' are also the group of people easily misunderstood and seldom understood, perhaps because of the complexities their life entails. In terms of age distribution, there seems to be a radical variation of opinions and this leads to a more comprehensive and complete approach to the issues at stake.

Credence to the noble words of Heraclitus the philosopher of change reveals that; "Out of what differs, comes the most beautiful Harmony".

Following this strand of reasoning some are of the opinion that a person is young from the age of 9 to 25. For them, it is the moment when these groups of persons are in their age of intensive dependency, on their parents, relations and teachers. Indeed, it is the age of people easily found in schools, wherever education is given due priority. They are those who depend on others to attain maturity.

Clarification of Concepts

According to a learned opinion of comrade Obunikem Asuzu, a former executive director, youth's orientation foundation Awka, in Eastern Nigeria. "The concept of who are youths' differs from place to place. As in Nigeria, like in most African countries it includes people between the ages of 12 to 30". Besides this, youthhood is a matter of the mental condition of the human person. As elders, who are physically and mentally agile even at the ages of 60 – 70 can still be said to be young.

A third group of analytic opinion says that youths' are also the group of humans who make the world happy by engaging in creative arts like drama, cinema, sports such as: in football, volleyball, and karat, boxing and racing. It is a stage that beckons on people to develop their talents, since only in using developed talents, can individual and collective abilities of people shine like stars to help illuminate the darkened territories of human destinies, often this is recorded in inventions of science and technology, which now help to make the world a better place, by alleviating the crude and brutish drudgery of state of nature.

Hence, almost all who fail to develop their talents constitute liabilities to their generation adding to the problems of life, when it takes only developed talents to solve and end almost every problem of this life.

This is true enough given all the statistics of Scientists, inventors and philosophers, more especially true, when we bring to mind the words of former American president, late John F. Kennedy who said that; "Every problem can be solved by man".

And in the opinion of the likes of, Ifeyinwa Agina and Julian Odogwu," youths' are those who go in for youth service for their father land, constituting the labour force in civilized nations". And "in Africa especially in Nigeria, up to 90% of youths' are victims of poverty". Generally, young people are often given to exhibition of uncontrolled emotion and many of them loose glorious fortunes because of this unrestricted inclination to emotional behaviour.

From sociological point of view, Youthhood starts from the age of 15 and lasts till 45 and at this stage; they are believed to be the working class people. And it is by end of this age that women attain their menopause and in this timely departure from youth-life, they can no longer bear children. By this classification the labour force and productivity of any country rest on their shoulders.

The last evaluative group believes that there are young mothers and young fathers and these remain young until the age of 60 for women and 65 for men. And it is in relation to this opinion that workers go on retirement at this age in many countries to give chance to younger group of workers.

Let us look at certain features of youthhood in an organized world:

A. Youth culture: is a direct reference to norms and

activities that are considered a common life style among the young people. This includes contemporary languages and slangs, high life music and modes of dressing both the moral and immoral.

B. Youth Hostel: Are cheap buildings often meant for students' overnight lodging as a traveler's accommodation for youths in developed societies.

C. Youth Quake: is a more important one, which aims to influence the youths' by bringing pragmatic change into the society, as in the famous French revolution crisis, and the most recent Arab youth revolution to remove era of chronic bad leadership of most Arab-Islamic nations. It is when youthful energy became the driving force to the cultural revolutions that bring serious change to human societies. It is in this context that some become radical and violent. This is pointer to the young people's riots in schools and villages, as a response to malicious element from elders' bad leadership. It is this bad leadership as common factor for lack of sufficient patriotism in nations, which we analyze.

To conclude this variation of age description, I believe that youthhood starts at the end of teenage. When one steps beyond the teenage life and it lasts until one-steps into old age. For at this moment one should not be called a child and still one is not an elder. Though, it is conventionally welcomed that at the age of 18, an individual is then capable of taking decisions, which often have to influence the rest of one's life.

It will therefore, become a modern science if parents can afford to invest about 95% of all the training they owe to give to their children before they can attain the age of 18, thereafter, allow their children to research the world, bringing from their childhood innate powers into youthhood, to help change the world for good.

This is because, undue influence of parents and families, can badly influence young people, often, hindering their talents from attaining development. Usually, experience show that many a youth are drifted from focusing on the development of the particular destiny they came to birth with, because of the self-interest of their parents, elders and ought to be mentors, these desire to determine for the youth what their future must be, choose their vocations in life for them, but none of these elders' received for the youth, 'the abiding' nature's inspiration and personal destiny revelation-guidance on how best to fulfill this destiny they came to birth with, when this happens, the young ones are left hanging and confused between the choices of divinity and humanity, this is one silent crisis in life that bring forth confusion in the life of the African youth.

All these are responsible for why there is some mental confusion leading to moral conflict among the young people especially in our part of the world, wherein in Africa, talents are poorly developed, underutilized and the developed ones, finding no proper appreciation at home, must be exported to Europe and America, and we open mouth to call this 'brain-drain', who then will develop Africa if this continues to happen?

Our political leaders often, out of leadership ignorance proclaim that they are inviting foreign investors to help us develop. These needs to wake up from political somnambulism because neither Europe nor America not even Asia got its development by inviting Africans to come and invest in their land. For all these foreign investors will end up exploiting the land in the continued spirit of imperialism, by further enslaving its citizens through unskilled labour without the essential transfer of technological know-how.

If you develop your homeland, the winds of nature will attract sufficient investors for you. China and Indian remain healthy examples for African nations to emulate. If Africans are sincerely ready for integral development as often claimed. Walter Rodney comes alive and handy here, when he argued in his book, 'How Europe Underdeveloped Africa', that; "development of any society is the sum total of re-investing of those resources, taken from the same society for its citizens welfare". Largely, this has not been so in the case of Africa, and this goes on and echoes in youth's memory, the economic crisis affecting the social and mental upbringing of the African youth.

Consequently, they have been left behind in contributing in technology and being known among the

C. H. Zudes

leading scientific inventors of this generation.

****

Youth is a progressive stage in life; it is the basic link between the stages of ingress and that of egress.

Ingress: is the stage of those coming into birth and it is the most primary stage of life, it is often referred to since, it gives rise to childhood, it becomes more important, because without it nothing will lead to youthhood. At this stage, the object is still a child, still flesh and anxious for existence.

Egress: is the climax stage of life, of which youthhood moves towards. It is a time when uncertainties of life seem dominant. This is the final stage in life, at this level; weakness due to old age shows more in life. And life's departure comes to focus. Indeed Egress is the end point of life to which the stage of progress which goes on in youthhood leads.

Progressive stage: Therefore, is that stage we see in youthhood. It is the most interesting stage in human life. It is a glorious opportunity that all desire to attain .The unwise wastes it, while the wise people strive to achieve so much with it. This is the stage, which those who have passed are regretting their wasteful past, while those who have not attained it are struggling to attain it. Also this stage is like flower of the tree of human life. When it has not blossomed it is not desired as beautiful. When it fades, its beauty is no more. While in between all

30

these, this is the most delightful stage full of splendor.

In youth's time, people are eager to love and be loved. People who believe in the wisdom of love continually share life as love for all people even in their old age. They believe that without love, there is no life as those who never loved, never lived.

By all this, it is a unique and rare opportunity in life. It comes and goes but those who do not live in awareness cannot notice its departing swiftness. This is why many still live in "had I known".

A conscious life makes one always happy and happy people seem younger than their age. This may be why the conventional humorous expression: "Every year young" is used to qualify some people. Infact, people unconsciously desire to be young or to be regarded younger than their age. Indeed, in some African countries, people are in the habit of falsifying their age especially to retain their position in the public service.

The Family:

The root of youthhood is most important and that is the family. The family is a home and is often made up of the parents, children and other relations. We have various kinds of family namely, The Nuclear, which is made up of father, mother and their children. The Extended family: is made up of parents, children and their various relations of varying degrees of paternal and maternal lineages. While in polygamous family, a father has more than one wife and consequently, there are likely to be many children. In the global society, some associations, groups and organizations, as in schools and Churches are other kinds of human family as they give shelter and function as agencies of socialization for the children and the youth.

The family as a home becomes the birthplace of a child. As a first wider world of children, it becomes an environment of care, shelter and socialization by means of learning. Here youths as children are sub – ordinate to parents, elders and available relations. It then becomes the primary duty of parents to reproduce, rear and care for children. But to what extent these actions are performed in African societies is the major concern of this book.

It is logically undeniable that the future of any human person owes its core to the initial influences of the family on it. Both the good and bad seeds are sown in human families. If parental care is properly undertaken in various family institutions, the youth will possess the best ability to build up his society. But it is clear that these obligatory duties no longer continued as the most rampant thing everywhere is child abuse. Consider then the music of Dr. Eric Oriedu; "Child abuse must stop!" children and youths are constantly abused by parents, Teachers and society especially in this neglect and abuse of politics and religion. This group is neglected and abused, but according to him "Child abuse must stop!! Yes for me too, 'child abuse can stop!!!'

Clarification of Concepts

Families neglect their most important duty on children. All they seem to care more for is one thing which is to keep on blaming them, as majority of the families have neither knowledge nor interest in the integral development of children. At homes and school, seldom are youths given sex education.

Why then is everybody ready to blame them when they make mistakes or commit shameful sexual scandal as often as they do in love affairs!

Youths are always the victims: They are denied respect (on their basic rights to be brought up well, but are still blamed for not giving the same respect they are denied. If respect is an ocean, that of most young people will be dried up by now, since they do not receive in return, the respect they have given out to elders). "Nemo dat quod non habet", is that Latin theory meaning "no one can give what he does not have, much more, when he/she never received it back".

From the elders who embezzle public funds, youth learnt the act of stealing. These elders came back to execute judgment, condemn and kill the young. They are debased and dehumanized; yet blamed for not being successful. Recent observations indicate that many families lack love, and seldom do you get parents who are ready to be friendly to their children. Being deserted, many children have taken refuge in illicit trading on the streets and especially on high ways. As many have abandoned education, how can their future be certain?

C. H. Zudes

In the opinion of Mrs. Ada Agbasimalo, the renowned author of the Nigerian Book: BOW YOU MUST; "Children's psyches are progressively affected negatively by parent's small doses of deceitfulness and lies". "The Child wants to go out with the parents and instead of explaining why the child cannot join the parents, the parents say to the child, go and bring my shoes for me" and before the child comes back from the errand, the parents have disappeared. This has a very negative effect on the development of children; it is a big way of destroying the psyche they bring into youth life.

"It is better to tell the child the truth, give him the reasons and let him start seeing you, the parents as credible. The child grows up to cherish credibility". The author said.

The government also engages in both child and youth-abuse, when they neglect Education by allowing industrial action of teachers, thus making our youths the victims. As seen in politics, religion and socio – cultural displays of events in human society. Neglect of Education and consequent abuse of youths in Nations are to be seen in their respective chapters.

WHAT IS JUBILEE?

Jubilee is a unique moment of remembrance of very important occasions in a lifetime. Generally, Jubilee is an official celebration of success, triumph or joyful reawakening of human consciousness, to God given opportunities in the past. It is a time of Joy, peace, hope and optimistic expectation for a more wonderful future filled with tantalizing promises and blessings.

In the understanding of Christian religion, Jubilee is a famous celebration indicating a prominent time of special indulgence. About age and time; people celebrate the Jubilee as a Jewel-like phenomenon surrounded with splendor, which are rarely found. This accounts for why at the noble age of 25, a Jubilee is titled a silver Jubilee, and at the unique age of 50, it becomes golden. While at the prominent age of 75 it is regarded as diamond. And at the rare glorious age of 100 a centenary Jubilee. In this context, it seems to have four major wings as it is measured by the on rolling of events up to twenty-five years.

Now, a Jubilee harvest in relation to African youths is a simple though intensive evaluation of life and love in and around the life of youths. It is more of a satirical exposition of immoral re-actions of people (elders) towards the youth. And this novel remains a Jubilee contribution of pieces of advice by a youth to other young ones not to imitate historical mistakes.

The writer herein, shares his first jubilee experiences in life with all men.

HOW, DO WE LOOK AT HARVEST?

When the word Harvest is mentioned, one of the first

things that occur to a rational person is a farmer whose time it may be to gather in the agricultural products of his field. Harvest may then be the time or season in a year when crops are gathered together and put into the barn. Harvest leads to abundance.... Our minds can also be stretched to understand harvest as a product of an effort. The result of one's labour, or action which has a reward. Harvest could then be seen as an after match of an event. What then is our harvest in relation with youthhood?

As in youthhood what we are going to see is a reference to human beings within a certain age of their existence, therefore when related to harvest, one may be gathering life experiences and challenges, depositing them in a barn like in this act of writing.

Though this age in question is within the scope of progressive maturity and continued development, one is both a learner and may be a learned person, who, being philosophically inclined stands to display and share with others the much wisdom he has gathered. Harvest extends to obtaining of result of behavior, it may thus be juxtaposed with an analytic approach to the events of life and love among the youths and their consequent result as well as the societal challenges they are bound to suffer from the elders, and malfunction of societal activities.

Yet under the scope of religion, harvest may also imply an event of thanks- giving. In all these, harvest comes last in a sequence of a given event.

Clarification of Concepts

THE CONCEPT OF "LOVE"

What actually is love? In the essential remarks of Green; (1964) "when the whole world lack peace, there is anarchy and war". And indeed, people are constantly searching for an important solution. When they find and practice this solution, profound order will naturally exist in the world. By such acts as this, no problem in the world will be insurmountable".

What then can this solution be? It is that universal concept called "love". How can we relate love to all the situations in the human society? And in the philosophic remark of Mr. Iyke Ojih, of Blessed memory, love is a product of two or more efforts. From this, when a man plants a seed and a woman water (nurture) it, it bears fruit; this fruit is "love". Love is that condition that makes peace and harmony possible.

Yet our inevitable enquiry remains; is love a physical or spiritual phenomenon? And where it is spiritual can it fully exist without a mode of physical manifestation? Where it is considered from the physical point of view, can its uniqueness and relevance be adequately communicated without tracing it back to a spiritual foundation? To consider love from the Religious background, one learns that under Christian evaluation, love is founded in God who is the transcendental love. An Igbo traditional religionist will measure love with ethical uprightness in man. In the Hausa like in the Islamic religion, love can also be measured in the practice of the 'Zakat', which means giving to the poor and the less fortunate. This is another way of showing that all humans are one.

Love is one factor that initiates equality among people, the truth is that all the problems and every war fought on earth is because people are seeking for how to communicate their unspoken urge for equality, whenever some arrogant humans claim the superiority that suggest the human society remains an 'Animal Farm of a kind,' as in gender right pursuit, the struggle for increment in salary of workers, leading to industrial strike actions, as a revolution against those who steal public funds, are all means to express zeal for equitable possession of properties with others. But in the absence of love, these things are done wrongly, creating chaotic episodes in society and only love can heal the problem that its absence creates.

But my question remains, how can we rightly associate love with sacrifice? If men regard sacrifice as a dominant feature in expressing love, how justifiable is that? Are all the modes and kinds of sacrifices actually an indication of love?

Then can love be felt where sacrifices do not exist? And can ritual sacrifices qualify as love? When one shades another's blood in ritual sacrifice for money, is such love? What are those basic factors that make love genuine and sincere in relation to the youths? When there is no passionate or sensual expression how indeed can they identify their loved or beloved one? To what extent have the young people been able to differentiate love from infatuation and concupiscent desires of the flesh?

For Joseph Fletcher; Love is classified in three kinds thus:

Filia

Erotic

Agape A

While for Ernest Oguguo in his book "LOVE IN FRIENDSHIP"

He classified love in six kinds thus:

(1) SENSIBLE LOVE: Is love arising from the senses, which enables man to do good to help both humans and animals.

(2) RATIONAL LOVE: Are loving actions, which are products of reason, which fulfils the fundamental objective of love.

(3) CONCUPISCENT LOVE: Is the lustful love built on strong desire, of an un-moderated kind? It concentrates on materialistic values. For this, many young people are victims and some have lost their fortunes and favours because of this theory of love.

(4) BENEVOLENT LOVE: this is the same with FILIA

Love and it is the good and obligatory love, which is conventionally accepted as genuine. It is the family love shared among parents, Children and Blood relations.

(5) **EROTIC LOVE:** Is the lowest kind of love in the degree of love. It is built on passion and emotional desire, often sensual sin is prompted by this.

(6) **AGAPE LOVE:** Is the fraternal love that exists among genuine friends. Popularly called Christian and God's love, which is Christ-like.

For me, love is a generous missionary; a strange visitor yet fills all who delight in it with joy. Love is a silent but unique creature. It is an invisible bond, an intuitional tie and a spiritual projection of an elastic blind link. This kind of link is what makes friendship and marriage possible irrespective of the absurdities involved. The natural link of love is what engenders the spirit to help and sympathy with others. It is by such link that unity and harmony give rise to peace.

BRIEF FACTS ON AFRICA

The Noble concept Africa is a continent comprising more of the most black people on earth and it is scientifically believed to be about 8 degrees away from the equator, making it the continent closest to the direct rays of the sun, this accounts more, for why most African people are dark or black skinned, given the direct intensity of the sun's rays on them. This is one of the five continental divisions of the world and it is made up of great ecological and environmental features that offer virginal wonders to minds of researchers.

"Africa and its people cannot be known without due consideration of its dominant features, which includes: its great size of land mass covering over 5,200 miles from Tangiers to Cape Town. Approximately the same distance from Panama City to Anchorage, Alaska. Also it 4600 miles from Dakar to cape Guardafui; In fact, Africa is as big as, about 3 times the size of the United States of America in land accumulation".

"It is a land of plateaus, swells and basins, prominent in its geographical and historic features. It is also surrounded by coastal plains all over its continent. And one of the earliest influences of Africa on the rest of the continents dates back to before the fifteenth century. As the first group of black people arrived America by 1494. Yet Africans had in 12th and 13th century, in its sub continent of south Sahara engaged in trading, its lands was flooded with cowries and currencies, as most people of African lands traded with the Romans and Greek traders even while Europe and America were still sound asleep in civilization, but only had to wake up in the 15th century A. D to exploit and disorganize the existing structures the Black people had created for itself.

Europe and even America thus were isolated then as Africa is now. Africa only has to pass through numerous stages of development and civilization again to come to the limelight of cosmopolitan civilization it projects today.

To consider its wide environmental features: It has been partitioned into five physical and vegetation zones, possessing an equal Mediterranean type of climate and arid plains. And on its parts close to the Equator were wide Savannah regions of widely covered grasslands and trees". More so, on the cardinal point perspective; Africa as a continent has been divided into four main categories: the North Africa: Which includes countries like Morocco and Algeria; the East Africans which includes: Ethiopia and Sudan, the West Africans: which includes Nigeria, Ghana and Cameron, and the southern Africans among which are found; Zambia and Angola. Considering the people of Africa, one will unavoidably take a lot of factors into evaluation thus:

(a)   What Africa is and what is its nature.

(b)   The numerous myths conferred as a mode of description of its people:

(c)   The idea of race and

(d)   The earliest basic business of the people:

Considering it response to natural world, the enormous populations of Africans were not as you would expect, it has still been un-able to connect with the societies of the world in the same pace of famous histories of civilization.

Clarification of Concepts

As a result, they became the victims of the easier developed world's intimidating, imposition of religion of strangers. Colonialism came handy as western and southern colonial masters came to it; these apparent masters were traders as a result of this, in exchange of the natural values of Africa, with the strangers' entangling gifts, the then rising economic front of the black race came to be devalued. Hence, following its character, which now determines its contemporary destiny, the Africa man came to be at the receiving end and it does seem he had received more than his nature's bargain was.

The several myths created and imposed on Africa; came to be the negative ideas of the missionaries, colonial masters and anthropologists, whose line of work includes acting as the colonial government officials and reporters. However, all seemed to have taken the advantage of African man's in-ability to explain himself and his natural values to disfigure issues to the extent of impoverishing the self-image of citizens of African continent.

They first regarded Africa as a 'dark continent' as was the opinion of the American and European visitors and workers and looked upon its inhabitants as specimens for physical and biological sciences.

By the 17th and 18th century, the myths of African continent as a savage land also became popular, they were upheld as a people who do not know about flames of civilization and are abandoned to the mercy of destructive forces of brute nature. Indeed, these were extensive mode of human disregard. And the missionaries who in negative consideration of their difficulties and harshness of African temperature in its closeness to the sun's rays, considered nothing better of Africa, but to kept this idea of timid life in their written works, thus it became a popular concept of Africa in most of human awareness.

However, today it was enough challenge for the younger generation of Africans to keep their banner higher in living out the quality of life that will at all times and in all things remain a total contradiction to these negatively exaggerated reports of the early missionaries and explorers. (Africans' should not bear a resemblance to this mockery made to it, as has so far been reflective in these porous manners of poor indigenous leadership offered by some wood headed politicians , in this unrepentant love to cling to power and diffuse the wealth of the continent).

Also, in one of the American assessment of the Africans, they looked upon Africa as a black race. However, they failed to understand that in Africa, everything is not black. For within it, there exists the Caucasians, the white race like in Morocco, Egypt and Algeria e.t.c. "It is then a very dishonest approach, for Americans and even Europeans, to have applied false scientific claims in moral evaluation of other continents".

Clarification of Concepts

Then, the legendary tales concerning the Black Americans, these ought to be Africans, who today compose part of the genuine American citizenship comes handy. As this cannot be isolated from the famous events of 1494, when earliest known account of Ancestors of Black Americans were first sold into slavery. It echoes a reverberation on today as part of historic confusion offered to the black race, since among their descendants can still be found variations of opinions, as they seldom accepted one particular opinion about their descent in relationship to Africa, and this reflects so much about its past devalued image. Yet this differentiation can even be turned to more positive opportunities, and lesser negative options as is seen in the opinion of Heraclitus the philosopher from Samos, in Ephesus that:

"Out of what differs, comes the most beautiful harmony", if only the younger generation among them decide to see themselves as youths of Africa, they will alleviate the burden their ancestors had carried on and help Africa alleviate the burden it carries on its shoulder, as a land whose heroes are in exile (examine this in the theory of the 'North Star')..

Therefore, while some welcomed Africa with loving ideas of great delight, some others did out of their challenging necessity of locating their cultural background. And the rest of them only did with high rate of personal interests in their personal dispositional mode of accepting the belief fate have associated them with. This is indeed a great burden to carry from life.

All these show the diversity in man's ability to think. It is then a progressive historic event that almost all Black Americans, now turn to Africa as a way of searching for their root. As today, African heritage in them are never lost. It cannot be denied then, that African heritage in them has adequately contributed to the upgrading and enriching of American culture, which is an exciting, and glittering object to all the worlds.

It is then encouraging to learn that pan-Africanism took root among them even in their famous strange-lands of their birth and this has its branches spread over Africa today. "As the French speaking Africans saw negritude, their taking delight in blackness as a rational and radical approach to correct these ancient wrong images. And as the American Negroes deny imposed myths by tending to build new ones, like the; I have a dream, of Martin Luther King jnr. that later gave birth to this day's era of Barack Obama becoming the first black president of America". All these constitute the vibrant and driving force in black revolution to better the ruined face of Africa. For it is only when the myths are wiped away that African realities can be known.

Therefore, in the views of Governor Rotimi Amechi of Rivers state in Nigeria,

"It is more important to create the reality, and images imposed against you will disappear".

Clarification of Concepts

What do you and I consider now as African reality? What do we create that the youth may raise this continent higher with it?

As we cannot avoid questioning what economic activities of Africans was, we cannot overlook the issues around slave trade, by which African humans were debased, devalued and dehumanized by their fellow one-headed humans. The slave trade is like a unique evil upsurge. Indeed, it was and still remains the zenith of absolute man inhumanity to man.

A renewed credence to the position of His Excellency, Late Chief Odumegwu Emeka Ojukwu, that; "the greatest problem of Africa is the injustice done to it, the self justice it is yet to achieve for its own people's emancipation, while Europe and America are only at vantage point because of self justice they achieved and the injustice no one has done to them" B.

In the written ideas of Philip D. Curtin he states: "In the decade after 1783, there the alternative of developing tropical Africa began to have the following".

"When European power (Britain) turned to Africa in 18 A.D. It was West Africa that counted most, as the region of commercial promise was that of existing slave trade. From Beneguela coast in Angola to the Senegal in later 1780's a total transport of about 75,000 slaves were sold yearly out of Africa".

And the relations between African political authorities

and Europeans trading the coast were that of casual partners in commercial transactions. (It is a pity to discover the nature of our problem, it seems innate, as it is the gerontocracy in our heritage that betrayed our journey to human destiny, making it longer than necessary as not all political elders can be faithful or patriotic in our land, some still betray Africa again, even now the question is why? In this we discover that, the European seldom raised issues of political sovereignty then C. But Africans suggested it to them in the body language of elders in our land.

Also, the literary ideas of Basil Davidson states further;

"Oversea trade in slaves was one which sowed disorder where ever it touched" "As it disrupted the peace and security which was prevalent in central Africa. Yet 19th century invaders of Africa understood all this as a tactics in their invasion. In reality, Europe struck Africa in its moment of great confusion. Pombeiros (Congo slaves) became agents of slave master's ill actions with Africa in those ancient hours of historic uncertainties. (It had been the crisis of a continent).

Apart from all these, there was also in Africa the ages of stone and Iron Technologies, these become the people's chief labour and Pre - occupation. Beyond it, from slaves who often laboured as farmers; truly, the introduction of ferrous (iron) Technology set in motion series of changes crucial for historical Africa of medieval times.

Clarification of Concepts

"As Neolithic began the age of metals, – Iron became most important of all metals. It was this metal technology that facilitated the notion of gods, government and custom, all these dates back to common source, the idea of entrenching order in human civilization".

Neolithic system flourished during the 4th Millennium, while stock raising system was taking root in the coasts of Africa. Then after this Stone Age, came the time of primitive invention of Agriculture.

It could then be known that for about 6000 years ago, people of the lower Nile Egypt had practiced and attained (better) achievements in Agriculture. Humanity was sparse in Africa at this era, from North of Congo basin to Cape of Good Hope, were scattered group of hunters, these like other Africans paid less attention to Agriculture.

A tangible fact remains that in General survey of African Societies, "African countries share many similarities in growth, close affiliation of languages, belief and social organizations, and thus they share much of their traits with Europe. As in food production methods, markets and families reflect great similarity. Africa tends often polygamous, exploited in areas of justice, imaged as one not capable of self determination, while Europe, Asia and America is free from African exploitation. They share a great pool of cultural similarities but different manifestations in exploitation of the black race, who too is a fellow human. It has taken more than a century to prove to the contrary this unfairness in claims and reference to Africa as an inferior continent D.

Every African especially the youth; shares the challenge of the golden age to make positive contributions to move Africa forward, bearing in mind how the immediate past generation laboured to achieve independence, a number of notable changes occurred between 1950 July – 1960. For about 1960's (African nations began to attain their independence) practically, many Africans had been trained to take over Administrations of homelands" to this Day but how well have these faired?

The present fading generation of leaders in Africa, has failed to keep history of self emancipation of black race alive, they are rich in nepotism. This is why the theory of brazing fire of corruption can be greatly associated to people and nations of this age.

The youth of Africa who must take over from this group can not under any guise be allowed to fail like fading politicians of our time. It is better and more honourable that the youth refer back to their ancestors, befriend and become friends of Ancestors, the heroes past, who laboured to bring the African independence. This is more honourable than any attempt to be a photocopy of the age when leading men has allowed corruption to flourish as if it is a culture. These men are lost in unfriendly capitalism of love power, which kills the

Clarification of Concepts

African spirit of unity formerly expressed in Ujama philosophy, (I am because you are), they debased that humanity in negritude, offered by President Julius Nyerere as the blackness in our race has not united us, but we presume the unity of our race only in the terms of those claims in support of what the strangers amalgamation had imposed in their own advantage. These were the elders of the white race, what have the elders of the black people chosen to their people's advantage?

In this work, we make a bold attempt to propose to the African youth to become friends of their good, golden Ancestors past. This is one thing that will put an end to the evil in our land, a pointer to self actualization and a re-incarnation of Africa pragmatism that upholds true nationalism through respect for patriotism.

CHARACTERISTICS OF YOUTHHOOD

"If you gathered nothing in your youth

How can you achieve something in your old age"? D1

"Youth is an opportunity to do something

 And become somebody" - (T.T. Munger).

The concept under study is not meant to be subjective in any way but by its diction, it is a concept of objective category. Therefore, we have to classify its dominant characteristics in two ways: the positive and negative characteristics.

Considering the positive characteristic's of youthhood, one have to bear in mind that it is a heroic opportunity, when one is full of strength, vigorous mental acumen as in the case of students boisterous force for action and in the cases of those whose lives challenges and business requires physical fitness.

On the abstract perspective, people at this age count more on beauty and handsomeness of one's existence. As the beautiful and handsome ones are easily desired and cherished. And those not naturally endowed with all these, artificially make it up in order thus to qualify for taste of people easily desired. Thus the splendid favored youth engage in beauty context competitions. There is also an advanced interest of youth to desire a lot of things among which includes factors like financial success and essential political empowerment in life.

The highly emotional minded group desire to love others and as much, desire to be loved in return and for such people, one good turn deserves another. Hence for such young people, love is all that counts in life when young. But the ascetical inclined youth care for one thing, which is success. It may be spiritually, mentally and academically. For this group, those who have not succeeded in life have not really worked for it, as those who work hard always succeeded, even when it is delayed, it must not be denied.

These days, many have seen the value of hard work and each man seems conscious of developing the talents imbued in man in other to realize a prosperous future. Today, many who work strive to become educated, as so many people create time to attend weekend lectures and a lot of other youth engage in skill acquisition in youth forum conferences. Actually, many people are working hard today yet for them, success seems uncertain, often because they live in an unjust society.

The students of many Nigerian universities in the student organization levels have as their motto: "Aluta continua victoria acerta" which means struggle continues, victory is certain, therefore, the spirit of youthhood here, is a challenge to all young people to do their own part conquer the injustice in all African societies. And in all these the young people's ambition is more of an attempt in the positive direction, to accomplish the unattained dreams of their predecessors. Infact, these indicate that some people are living in awareness and awareness is the best positive characteristic to make a happy and fulfilled youth's life.

And in the realm of the negative characteristics, we shall look out to outline and consequently correct the non-relevant qualities which some youth often display, while being ignorant of their future detrimental implications. Generally, stubbornness is an outstanding dangerous character, which many young people feel at home with. And because of this, a lot of the elderly people have concluded that the youth are incorrigible and for this reason find it difficult to help the young people when need for such help arises. As in the remark of the Nigerian author Mrs. Ada Agbasimalo: "The youth in the university should desist from thinking that they know everything and cannot be corrected."

Nobody knows everything, and when you admit that you do not know, your system becomes ready to learn and take corrections. The youth should then learn that wise people learn more from the corrections applied to the mistakes of other people, this kind of learning from a distance is an act of genius, but waiting to make your own mistakes as the only way you can learn, means you are poor in acquiring knowledge through perception and absorption.

Also many young people do a lot of harm to their prominent future by following bad gangs, forming bad habits. Among these dangerous and self destructive habits are the: Inclination to drug addiction, chain smoking syndrome, drug pushing business and allowing oneself to be bought over as a hired assassin. Also there is this wrong notion of politics in both family and the state, the youth are still bought over as tugs, bad boys and easily ensnared into ancient enmities, which they often know nothing about its origin. It is both shameful and pitiable, for this mode of self-annihilation to be continuing among the youth in and around the African countries. For this is another way by which the youth, still take instruction from the same people who destroyed the world and made it almost impossible for anyone to enjoy living in it.

Now, like the biblical Esau, many young ones are carelessly selling their birthrights for the cheap and sordid money that brings them no blessed joy.

We should learn that a righteous life is an easier way to become rich if indeed one is sincere to oneself and determined to improve on ones weak points in life. This is the architect of all the factors, besides the devastation done by politicians, which as in those remark of Lady Julian Odogwu, up to 90 percent of the African youths are still victims of poverty, so many others languishing in penury of prison lives, unjustly because they have no body to stand in for them.

I have once seen an African 'rich-man in 2008', because he is a government servant, a Tax collector. He merely took advantage of his position as one paid salary in the service of a government, where youths are not cared for, to send some young people to the police Cell over a weekend, abandoned them there and refused them any chance of being heard or bailed, just to express that he has powers, and is better than others. This is brute capitalism, today being privileged and the unemployed youth who struggled to do business around his premises can be wrongly accused, charged as thieves and condemned just like that. This has gradually becomes a people's culture. In this way many youths are in the prison, but unlike this man presumed, God delivered those thus accused some hours later through superior connections as it is best understood.

Another way by which some youth do a great harm to their blessed future is by copying the bad examples, as in these injustices and a lot of abominable evil practices from the older generation.

Every youth should endeavour to read the book: Skeleton of Ancestors, by Timothy Ofoegbu they can from it learn much on how best to have nothing to do with some of those obsolete phenomenon of negative ancestral origin, often presumed as culture.

The last but not the least of negative characteristics is the consistent credence of some of the youth, who are often given to ignorance at the expense of wisdom through the uncontrolled passionate desires and motivations in their life.

Drunkenness is a lower value for life and inadequate reasoning as to attain reliable solutions in a given problematic situation. Many have carelessly wasted what they could have preserved, if only they were careful. In fact, the greatest canker worm that devalue our nature's rich value imbued upon all is our rampant mode of existing without the fear of God.

Clarification of Concepts

Though man is an intellectual being, but greater part of his actions indicates that many people love ignorance more than knowledge of the good life. The youth should then rely more on fear of God, which gives the greatest credence to wisdom. This alone, can make life better.

It is important to point to the fact that many are poor, others are begging in their old age, many are very sick and hopeless simply because of the level of careless lives they lived in their youth. Even if you are rich in your youth, what matters is; what sacrifice/ investment do you make for a successful old age?

What fire wood did you gather? What help did you render to help make the world a better place? What skill and knowledge did you gather, to qualify you as a reputable model of the young, or do you think that every elder even the evil geniuses are models to life, simply because they bear grey hairs?

C. H. Zudes

TWO | Harvest of Life and Love

African youth are today faced with obligation to rise up to the challenge of a life of conscious existence. The truth is, many fortunes have been lost in the young people's life and multiple opportunities not utilized to make their world a better place. Many odd things have been and still go on happening in Africa and above all in Nigeria. Not because they are good or reasonable, but because we inherited them. "These were our noble heritage from our fore fathers" is often the claim. Yet, they are the cause of our ruin and hindrance in the annals of historic development and advantageous competitions among continents of the world.

Our sorrow continues not because they cannot stop, but the greatest unfortunate episode is that the youth' are imitating mistakes. They are gradually developing minds for adaptation to inimical phenomenon like politicians stealing from the public funds in human society. But why this-inter generational transfer of iniquity, an unwise repetition of negative trauma among the black people?

African youth are born for a nobler life of heroic adventure, for a glorious love of undiscovered fortunes. Think twice, beyond this restricted nature of ours!

Going beyond yourself, you discover in each human

consists a noble creature! "Similarly, a young mind, I am a complete embodiment of unquantifiable fortunes". By now, the youth' in our lands should learn by obvious rationalism to work for those glorious fortunes unattained by our predecessors. We must build our minds to overgrow these ignorant shadows our minds have inherited.

Oh youth, we must go for gold. Those golden fortunes undiscovered in our continent. Not so many Africans are going for gold in this soil. Our friends are still day-dreaming, some drinking the wine that will daze them into greater poverty and our brothers and fathers are ruined without justice in the prisons of our home lands. But only few selfish people are getting satisfaction in these lands of our domicile. Some are selfish leaders who have neither love nor regard for our lives. Yet greater majority are suffering, wretchedly, dehumanized and dying. Abandoned at the expense of essence, of existence our brethren are languishing in numerous prisons of life. Numerous Africans are beggars and we are to this day, cheated by brothers of the same black colour. Beyond the recommendation of our noble nature, as similarity of blood, is not going to save us. For many of the youth' are worse than exiles in the land of their birth. Neither right nor left is clear to them and so the leading men blur the future in Africa.

"How long shall it last this man's inhumanity to man among us? Unworthy to mention that many people still die of hunger, kwashiorkor and daily frustration in a blessed soil, sufficiently endowed to support the material needs of the entire human race. While only the selfish, few consume what belongs to us all".

Is the historic civil war still raging in our lands? Is silent slavery and wickedness the way to wisdom? Or is tribalism's abuse of essence of politics the solution and approach to the problems in our lands. Or shall these problems never be solved? Is slave trade continuing in Africa? It seems that the western colonizers had not gone. It seems that our people learnt only their wrongs. As if Mary Slessor had not come. As if our brothers are our co – colonizers. But shall the youth' in Africa continuously be slaves? For while in history it was abolished ambition is that noble freedom be given to all people and justice done to all men. But are Africans still far from this justice? Why then, this reckless imposition of deadened theories and selfish hypocritical ideas in government as the mortal causes the death of fellow mortals!   Is it by fighting tribal wars and religious conflicts that African countries will rehabilitate its devastated ruins?

There are silent wars in the families, wars in the Churches, greater wars in the senate, federal and state houses of representatives of the present democratic Countries. Wars in Kuwait, wars in Namibia, and another go on in Rwanda, now Boko Haram seems like a Jihad war beginning with northern Nigeria, when the same elders who ruined the world are using the youth of Africa to advance the selfish political frontiers of ancient evil fires. This carnage of blood-shed is not new to this soil, for since 1966,the archives of history show the facts indicating that this land has drank more blood than any other, may be blood mining and drilling will soon become a new business, like oil-wells, beginning in these regions of blood-bath. Yes because while the leading men are pretending that they cannot quench this evil-fire in the hands of the youth, the same create the picture that there are no elder-statesmen existing in this regional oligarchy, fanned with frames of bloodbath.

For if it was in South Eastern Nigeria, statesmen will stand up to stop evil as it took only the like of His Excellency Chief Emeka Odimegwu Ojukwu to quench the apparent prevailing bloodshed in the fight between the Aguleri and Umuleri people of Anambra state. Also, it took only the like of His Excellency Chief C.C. Onoh both of Blessed memory to quench the apparent prevailing blood bath between people of Abor 1 and those of Abor 2 both of Enugu state. While in South Southern Nigeria it took only the likes of Elder Edwin Clark to prevail on the Niger-Delta youth to cease-fire and sew for peace with the Government of His Excellency President Umaru Musa Yar'adua who offered the youth amnesty. Indeed, only this type of brave minded elders can be heroes and mentors to the young people of any progressive nation.

And why must there be political ways of depriving human freedom of worship, to deprive basic human freedom of existence and movement as in Sudan today?

Harvest of Life and Love

Think of zamfara, Jos and Kaduna sharia crisis of 2000/2001 in Nigeria. History is repeated negatively in our Continent, when in Borno and Kano in Northern Nigeria, one superlative invention is how to continually shed the blood of fellow black brothers and sisters under any guise, religion and otherwise. Is it that the only scientific invention coming from Nigeria to the world is this echo of blood-shed we have called it 'Boko Haram?'

Heroes must arise to oppose and stop evil any other thing is political ignorance.

We shall not forget that many African people have fallen sick and had steadily died, only in the name of incurable evil. Those who died out of our societal carelessness and culture of neglect to all that is essential, these could have helped to make our world a better place, when the deepest realities reveal that abuse of knowledge and application of ignorance is our only problem? But many think that we are poor. The youth' should learn to carefully harvest their fortunes knowingly and unknowingly hidden in this life of exile that is ours.

It does seem that the majority of African youth' are existing like people in exile. For wherever a man lives, and he is not treated like a citizen there lies his exile. Great people make greater fortunes in their exiles. As only in this can one be really great. Greatness is good; exiles are good, only for those, who sincerely try to be good. They can discover their fortunes in it. 'Youth' if you live in an exile do not be afraid to make your fortunes, for in such lay the greatest of opportunities. Let every man think of his fortunes, as every woman should conceive hers. As we think less of life's problems, let every African think of it now for there are so many fortunes in Africa.

The youth everywhere make their fortunes, making hare when the sun is shining. Let the youth in African countries be allowed to make their fortunes. For fortunes are never foreign to Africa. If the leaders will lead us to our fortune and the directors, direct us to these fortunes, God imbued us with talents these are to be funded as a mission of those in governance, such that even when exiled from public life, it may still be avenues to success in one's life.

 Those who know this are often patient and will make for one wherever they see it. American youth' are making fortunes. European youth' are studying theirs. Asian youth' are going towards their fortunes. Did they believe our youth have fortune in Africa? There are some fortunes in Africa and it is better to make it while you are young, by keeping busy always doing what it is right. Never allow yourself to waste. Do something good, at least while you are young.

Youth' of Africa do not fear to go into exile for in this are found divine lasting favours. Youth is not meant for emotion or passion only, as many who get busy drinking and smoking around express, each time they are asked;

Why do you smoke?

Do you not know that even the

manufacturers have to you that

smoking will make you die

earlier than your time?

They simply answer, "It is a habit".

Some claim that something must kill somebody in Africa. But are you here just to live and die. What of that assignment / problem of our people that only you are given the talent to solve on earth?

Who then will solve it? St. Paul advised; "Remember the assignment you were given, try to carry it out".

All personal bad habits must be brought under control and be changed. That is why you are given power of reason and intelligence, which differentiates you from lower animals abandoned in state of nature. Every cultural being like man, has ability to stop their bad habits. Take it hard and hash to reduce the animal nature in yourself when you are young that is the only way for greatness in life. 'Nothing good comes easy' they say! The youth need to be encouraged to do the above, bearing in mind the words of Oliver Goldsmith which states;

C. H. Zudes

"Organize your thoughts,

control your emotions

and you ordain your destiny".

****

For easiest missions may not lead to a blessing. As king Solomon never went into an exile, or any battle field; that may be why he fell from wisdom to women. Easy fortunes never last as well as those who make it never went on an exile. "In this exile of one's youth, it is better not to assume things, humble yourself to achieve greatness, do not assume you are already great or prosperous great people are unassuming".D2

Here, we dwell together in our exile, hoping a day will come to brighten our blackened fortunes in African soil. They had no regard for our youthful fortunes. That they showed no compassion for our splendor to last! They wasted the destiny bestowed on us without regard!

Today's youth in most African countries live in a world already betrayed by elders in the name of partisan politics. These have eaten the sour grape of human destiny. They raped the future of the nations, destroying every ligament of compact humanity that ought to establish a world of peace and progress, in this pretended unity of a powerful great nation as in the case of Nigeria, where endless number of diverse ethnic nationalities can dwell together as one people for the future destiny of their nation's prosperity.

What are left for the youth are the fragments of underdeveloped savannah grass lands and desert regions which give a sense of jungle life where the young must take the leftover of these fragments of humiliated human destiny by force. The youth are now revolting in various tribal fronts they are pushed to shed blood for their hatred for the inimical actions of the grey hairs. They are seeking nothing but more responsible political representation and leadership. It is simply the absence of this that generates and sustains the problems of people in Africa.

Yet another irony is that this pretended unity of diverse people has provided a comfort zone for most elders and politicians to find a hiding place for leadership irresponsibility where this magnanimity of diversity is the ember fanning the flames of corruption. While given the flowing waters of ethnic sentiment, every corrupt leader is spared, lest his own people will feel or cry out against marginalization, if their apparent brother is held to account for his stolen wealth.

This appears like a non-pragmatic episode, a case of stepping one's two legs into the mud-spattered chamelion feces which makes movement inconceivable. Progress and concept of successful nations are better understood from this analogy of an intelligent ant, whose smallness enables it to climb to highest heights, succeeding in its mission than an elephant whose only problem is its presumption of being the giant, that biggest of all animals, and its size hinders it from moving forward.

As if the ancient python has once more , swallowed the diamond of ancient-unity highly needed for progress, the same aged python is now asking the younger generation; "where is your or the unity?" At the same time, blaming the youth if what they, the ancient's hands have politically disunited should be socially divided, in this confusion, anyone who point's direction is accused of being guilty of sabotaging nationalism, but only this direction in itself is nationalistic in the first place.

In their actions lay no love, they destroyed every principle of unity! Today,

….In their daily preaching a speech on love! What a grand pretence about unity.

They had no patience to spare our lives, sending us into an exile to wander without destination.

Today's young people must truly admit that challenges in life are never easy to overcome. Yet always, there are things that consoles if you remember that favours go before him who fears his God! Divine Splendour speaks for him, before his foes. Those who lack regard, lack love. But only one thing easily comforts. For as fortunes exist, so do friends in one's exile. There are more friends than enemies in life. I am happy that no man can qualify for an enemy. Do not fear them who treat us as enemies.

Let us conquer them and make them friend, "for better the man who have no enemies than the one who have no friends".

Tribalism in Nigeria is a business that has no friends. Therefore, tribal political-war merchants should stop and tell the youth the truth. Which is that selfless development of their entire regions as one universal family without religious or political claims is a better alternative to progress in Africa, if not, no one should pretend to defend the unity of any people when the falsehood in this claims of unity hinders the progress of the giant.

C. H. Zudes

THREE | African Youths of Today

It is wrong to think that the youths of today are corrupt. The simple truth may rather be that the youth in almost every generation learn or inherit almost all corruption from the elderly. Some also think that the youth of our time are too bad, the basic fact remains that "those who have not seen life become so judgmental" (Anon).

"Youth of nowadays" is a common expression in the lips of many people. Yet critical evaluations of these orators indicate that they are the pessimistic type who seldom believes that something good can exist in the life of others. They push a young man to the wall and still expect him to be gentle in battle of life. Who are those who sow the seed of sorrow in the heart of men and clap for them to smile, and if they indicate sorrow, will still blame them for accepting sorrow.

Our youth are victims of hypocritical ills and sorrow of their societies. In these they are born. In it they are brought up and blamed. Yet of these they are restricted and banned never to overgrow lest they will be misunderstood.

However, some youth are not innocent, as these have chosen negative ancestral footsteps by accepting to play the evil game transferred from bad parents. These improve on these ancient evils and corrupt other youth

71

by gradual influence.

In this remarks of H.R.H Igwe Austin Ezenwa in his political Risorgimento, "who says that the world is in danger? Surely not in the opinion of great minds, not in the life of wise ones" Who then thinks that the youths are very bad and why do you think that, they cannot contribute better in revolutionalizing the world even as they live in it, why do you still say they have no experience?

What then have the grey hairs with all these experiences done to make the world a better place?

The youth are at the heart of their world's abuse of values. In Africa we need to be sincere to ourselves, for our present day youth have continuously been victims of political cum military violence of society in which they were born. Our people seem to forget that, what they are taught is what they practice. We must remember that majority of the African societies have existed long, under a state of military manipulation of politics and some civilian's participation in sycophantic ideologies, it is then necessary to understand that the youth can hear more of the language of command. And those who have no hope must struggle to survive, as the strongest instinct in life is self preservation. And this is how the leading men teach the youth of today how to practice evil. For their conscience steadily preaches; "this wealth of the nations unwisely spent, employment unjustly given or denied still belongs to us all.

African Youths of Today

Majority are hungry, others are painfully sorrowing, seeing the unhealthy- hungry Africans dying, they cannot help coping with the bare minimum that prevents them from starving. It is a Bitter sorrow in every sincere heart; if we accuse the dying, even force them to die all in the name of law, security and leadership without considering the truth, when their only action is that struggle to survive. Can a good government call its citizens thieves?

There is a theory called situational ethics; it is a factor that morally justifies a person, even if his/her action was considered an offence against existing laws. A good example is a case where a dying person takes or steals a loaf of bread valued a ten naira. If the aim is to survive and not die of hunger, this action under the study of jurisprudence (philosophy of Law) is not a crime. This is further true, because the first instinct in human and in life is self preservation.

This why even in the Holy Bible, the command of God to the Israelites about harvest is to reserve some portion of the lands produce in the farm for the needy, the poor, the hopeless and the orphan. It is the same God's law that gave birth to universal law. It is from this universal law that every other constitutional law of countries took their origin, even the American constitution. But in our land today, we have killed youths, shot others, by the police or other uniform men. These may be, they stole bread or water or meat; they are accused, beaten, jailed or even killed, find out the conspiracy against common

73

humanity that happens in Abattoir Abuja. The government, police etc goes to the news paper to prove that catching a poor thief means they are working hard.

These same institutions are very silent, closing their ears from hearing of the crimes of the so called rich, the Oil baron and every so called grey-hair, who have stolen the nation blind by storing the wealth of fellow Africans in Europe, and America, especially in Switzerland. What have these uniform men done against these evils of those who claim to be rich?

The first thing the young victims of poverty often receive from society these days is a gift of undeserved blames. They are easily subjected to things they do not rightly belong to. And everybody thinks they are the worst humans if they are found stealing. Others think they are the worst sinners, when they fall victims of immorality. When they perform badly, perhaps in school, they are easily dehumanized, and treated with famous lies that they are not intelligent. A historic echo of ruining lie is told against the young, even among religions.

As the men chosen to be shepherds over them will now claim, these devalued youth' have no business being with them". Have they forgotten their holy mission among humans, where are we going?

Our lives have become a longer journey to approaching the human destiny. It is time our people should grow in understanding that nothing is wrong with the youth except that the societies in which they are born have no God conscious and God-fearing leaders.

Consequently they are leading the innocent youth' to godlessness and adventure into wickedness. Those who are so comfortable with condemning the youth should think twice and note "there are still the best of it in the worst of us and there are still the worst of it in the best of us".

What then have you done to make this world of ours a better place?

"Live then in such a way that you have something to contribute, after all what matters is what you contributed" says. – Dr. Bona-Christus the Philosopher.

When you condemn the youth who are thieves or who revolt against the insincerity of leading men and direct police to shoot at sight, are these youth not born with equal glorious destinies like all men? Or is it because very few are fortunate today. The wealth stolen to foreign nations and the much money wasted in paying the security forces; even when the greatest security is doing and insisting on justice to all citizens, when we fail in justice, we hide our ignorance and leadership weaknesses in this pride in spending spuriously in security, imagine the so called security votes of our state governors, can't much of these create employment and salvage the youth from lawlessness? While in them lay the greatest potential to help make the best of contributions to development. Politicians must always remember that from the ancient hours of politics, "There will never be peace in any state unless philosophers become leaders (and) or leaders become philosophers" – Plato.

Why are some busy condemning the immoral behaviour of our youth? Do their parents teach them much about moral or sexual dos and don'ts? At homes why do our people think that all parents know the right and correct thing to teach at all times? Is it not superstitious to think that to teach children much about sexual education is to corrupt their manners? Why are they corrupt as they are never taught? "Teach your child what is right and when he grows he will never depart from it" E.

Why do they think that the youth who have not performed well academically today are the never do wells? And easily they claimed that they are not intelligent, who told them? Did they examine properly before they Judge the African youth? Without patient and proper critical evaluation of everything about our youth', who says that there is justice in this attitude of proving to the youth' that they do not belong in this, without precisely showing them where they belong?

Often those positioned to determine the fate and future of the African youth are not those best qualified to do these works with love. These lacks of love is destructive to our world. The concept of the African youth has much to do with African destiny, for they cannot devalue the youth and think that they are developing Africa.

For once the African leaders cannot keep the youth so busy with noble events, it is certain that the elders, the politicians are destroying the present in order to deny the future. For once a young person is idle; such a one is bound in conscience to find ways of spending their energy. But often these become the bad ways. As in youth, lie glorious strengths. Why do you make of them, drug addicts and chain smokers when you created no employment for them, or even swept their feet off the existing carpet they had stood upon?

Indeed, this becomes part of negative characteristics of youth of today. While the positive ones are that youth' are struggling, studying harder now and desiring to make better their future than their parents ever made in the past.

There is much we are losing, by understanding the youth for what they are not. And much lies we are telling by denying of them, what they are better in need of at specific times in history. Elders and high-ranking professionals, who neglect children, are destroying the greatest need for which life is actually made. And those who think and often believe that youth are bad or wayward, should understand today that every youth is still ready to live a good life, but how and from where can they learn to practice it, if the human society is continuously praising those elders who lay the bad foundations or give credence to the evils in the society .The future destiny of Africa is in the youth' for the future of any nation is in the hands of its youth.

If Africa plans for a great future destiny like the rest of the continents, what do its leaders make of its youth today? What shall they inherit for, imagine this words of Seneca, the Philosopher;

"What madness it is for a man to starve himself (Neighbour) to enrich his (Descendants) and so turn a friend into an enemy! For his joy at your death will be proportional to what you leave him".

Let all who are political and religious leaders examine themselves in the mirror of these words.

Have they spent their time in destructive adventurous making episodes? Did they sin against this noble soil of unharnessed fortunes? Is it true that our past heroes had planted the good seeds, but not many are here to water them today? That in their time our past heroes cared so much, but little care is sufficient for leading people today. The idea of neither ready nor courageous is our problem. For people who are ready to do good are not courageous and the few courageous ones are seldom ready to do good.

In these African mountains, are hidden our destinies as the valleys the past heroes never levelled are left unlevelled today. Are the bulldozers no longer here or that farming tractors do not function efficiently again? The past heroes did well to harvest our fortunes, as they are gone, who then builds our lands? As our ruins are many and some primitive aspects still remain. Are we humans or cannibals? Who have taken much delight in ruining another's brother and have given no credence to the death and groaning of his own brothers. It is as dangerous as ignorance to be king in time without developing one's fatherland in hope of a better future and the welfare of your own people and kin.

What a great pity that African soils are still underdeveloped. Almost everywhere in our lands remains bush land. Is ours a society of animal jungle, or do we campaign to be called bush-men? As our heroic minded youth have no political powers and no money, they lack people and lack governmental positioning. These have no police and no protection. Our youths should do well to wake up the qualitative behaviours of our past noble ancestors. Never let us feel free to imitate the sinful attributes of our present deprivation.

The truth remains that our people are so slow in imitating Justice. How many fat foreign bank accounts were unjustly developed at the expense of multitudes of human lives? Do you care to know how many equal humans who suffer and die because of this silent and secret wickedness of yours? The youth whose life and future are at stake are the major victims. And after you have built skyscrapers in London, have you given a home to fellow homeless Africans? Have you assisted the sick that your actions have brought ruin and downfall? Have you fed the hungry African youth? Did you provide for their needs? Whose money, is it not theirs? Or do you think you are the only favoured human because you are chosen to serve and save your own brothers? So you end up in betrayal. Imagine yourself on these roads to anti-heroism—some have built tunnels into the sea, while others have carried the wealth meant for their own father's soil to develop again the most developed parts of the worlds.

Jubilee Harvest of Life for African Youths

They left their own father's soil a wretched and destitute domain. Indeed this wickedness is destroying the noble-minded youth of Africa. They use African money to buy Africans, buying the lands of Europe and purchasing the sea harbours of America. They bought over our youth and some cheap-youths are their sycophants. They are training youths to shed their own brother's blood. Why? They make youth assassins of innocent courageous Africans. But is Africa not worthy to own innocent courageous citizens?

And everybody is going to Europe to rest on a vacation; but do Europeans and Americans come to Africa for vacation or rest? When people think they are smart, they do not know they are in their self-sent exile, digging and decorating flowers in their own grave yards.

They bought over our youths, and made slaves of their own brothers when they employ them as bodyguards. Many have paid with their own blood. Is that a heroic personality? For heroes do not need bodyguards. Is their ambition to grow richer than their own countries? Are they actually rich if the country that is their homeland is getting poorer every day? Are they actually rich, if they cannot solve the youth's problems and make them into better persons? No man came out with riches and none will go back with them. They appear to be what they are not. "Appearance deceives reality". Oh my fellow mere mortals stop deluding yourselves. For "whatever is, had been, and shall be again. Nothing is new under heaven."

C. H. Zudes

Who actually aims to alleviate his own brothers' problems? And yet they teach us of African brotherhood?

Yet, every human problem is meant to be solved. Who can bear to be hated provided that justice is done and goodness flourishes, knowing that goodness is its own reward, then he is a Hero. For "in his days; Justice will flourish and peace till the moon fails" F.

What this generation lack, and needs most to resolve the crisis besieging humanity, is people who will constantly fear God and who will never ensnare their neighbours. They should be aware that our world is bound to consist of multiplicity of radical opinions. - That our world is a complex parallel citadel to contain anything that cares to exist in it. Including opposition of opponents. They must never shed blood. This liquid treasure thicker than water is too precious for any human to waste.

Our people must learn to avoid jealousy, which weakens the rational ability of man. Only a man who tells himself the basic truth can be happy, as it requires heroic courage to be a good man in this life. If people can call a spade, a spade, and determine to know that evil is evil no matter who does it, it surely merits a chain of repercussions. If our people can remember that the "fear of God is the beginning of wisdom, that to depart from evil is understanding and those who do so prove themselves wise" G. And that by avoiding evil, humans are liable to purity of ideas with which no problem can lack solution. But where shall our determination start?

If our youth consider Ferdinand Magerund in his circumnavigation of the earth, he never counted his opposition. Can we also not consider Christopher Columbus in his uncertain journey, which discovered the south Indies! Which becomes today's America. He paid no attention to wretched, unwilling to work advisers. He was determined to and he succeeded in founding the most prominent country in the world. Imagine James Watt in the world's history of electricity he was holistically conditioned in radical optimism without which our world may never know electricity. What have our African youths or elders been able to found?

A happy youth should never be distracted by oppositions, but learn from its message, often they are necessary! Great Heroism comes through simplicity of human determination to do the right thing without fearing oppositions but learning from historic mistakes of other men.

Education when it is integrally applied remains the most vital instrument through which youths can be equipped with the basic and fundamental audacity of mind to work out their life's needed solutions.

FIVE | African Elders and Heroes

The idea and the term elder bring to mind that some people are old while others are young. Consequently, elders are old people of bi-sexual category. This may consist of the parents, relations, and sponsors, directors, leading or titled people in the human society. Yet, generally, they are people older and not younger than the youth. Elders are naturally positioned to take care of the youth socially, religiously and otherwise. They help as teachers, caretakers and advisers who help to improve the level of knowledge in the life of the youth. And a good elder in African society is meant to be a guardian to all the youth'. Following the empirical belief of our people, that knowledge comes from experience, young ones acquire knowledge by learning from experience often.

A hero is an admired personality who is loved and cherished for his brave actions. Heroes are great minds, who accomplished royal adventures. They take part in events as prominent characters of useful value. As in a literary act, plays and films, the heroes are the main characters whose actions influence much of the activities in the play. Therefore, heroes are those characters who make things happen the ways they happen. Hence, no episode in human history will be complete without recounting its heroes.

C. H. Zudes

Consequently, African history will not be complete without giving credence to the positive activities of the past heroes among whom are some elders, worthy of emulations by today's youth'. But in many prevalent situations in the society, the opposite of all these tend to come about, as not all the elders in our society can qualify as heroes. For many who ought to gather our scattered Sacred Stones are actually scattering them the more. It is a pity that for the youth, life is no longer at ease. As ought to be guardians are guarding none.

And many are ignorant who need to guide us while some who are not ignorant are lost in selfish pursuit of vanities.

The heroes did well to harvest our fortunes; they fought it out with the white men. They never got bowed down until justice was done. Woe still remains, for everything seems to stop where they stopped as the goods they never did were politically done wrongly. For in spite of their imperfections they proved that man could still achieve justice towards fellow men. Can any African be justified to forget the selfless actions of people like: Rt. Hon. Dr. Nnamdi Azikiwe, first Nigerian president, Dr. Kwame Nkrumah of Ghana, Dr. Julius Nyerere of Tanzania and Chief Obafemi Awolowo of Southern Western Nigeria who aimed at massive education for the youth of his time?

And people like Alhaji Tafawa Belewa of Northern Nigeria? Can we forget of Gen. Muhamed Buhari and late General Tunde Idiagbon of Nigerian Army, who laboured to sanitize and discipline their fatherland Nigeria, or Gen. Chukwuemeka Odumegwu Ojukwu, who led the Biafran civil war against the sprouting seeds of corruption in Nigeria? Most of the elders today, were among those who ignorantly sabotaged his efforts, it seems that heroes are no more and today corruption is grown up. Where are the heroes of our time?

It does seem none still exists? If not, why is there so much evil in our society even at the expense of justice, peace and progress? And no one is opposing it.

In the opinion of late Bishop Godfrey Okoye of Enugu Catholic Diocese in Eastern Nigeria is both fundamental and consistent that;

"All that is required for the triumph

   of evil in a society is for the wise men

     to keep quiet, in the face of evil".

Most elders are so bowed down in selfish existence that so many are no longer models. The examples they display for the young are not worthy of emulation. As any attempt in copying such actions makes one become immoral, corrupt, depraved and fraudulently wayward as well as holistically un-patriotic. In African countries, many have departed from the path of wisdom. Elders are making the youth of Africa certain to wallow in sorrow and greater tears than life has made natural.

The youth' need to brace up to these ordeals for even as daily realities reveal "Life is not a bed of Roses," that suffering is path of worthwhile existence. This may be acceptable, but in wisdom, man must reasonably differentiate the abnormal from what ought to be. In our daily dilemma of life, African youths seem to receive the double portion, of ills, which in truth they never bargained for. He\she is a being in between warring realities. The youth is like the ordinary grass sprouting off the earth, which suffers when two great Elephants fight. In life, they exist as the silent participants in events between divinity and humanity particularly the elders and true human destiny.

Elders are naturally good yet not all of them are. Indeed they can be the repository objects of empirical wisdom. They are often the embodiments of noble cultures. However, rational and critical observations reveal that for elders to be generally good to the youth as natural moral obligation implies, our elders need to be less African in ideology. Their concept and outlook towards children and the youth should change for these are grossly and inimically under rating and devaluing younger people. This is massively hindering the development of our countries.

In Africa, there is still that obsolete mode of apparent child abuse. For many believe so much in gerontocratic system of existence and governance. In cyclic or spiral system of thought and in polychromic system of timing, giving rise to the so-called 'African time', perhaps responsible for its people's underdevelopment. These may be good for some, but for any reasonable youth they remain obsolete and needs to be updated. As there are more modern and scientific things much better than those in our world today. In fact, many in African life pattern make one to believe that we are going back while the rest of the world's reasonable creatures are getting more advanced in their present, while building their nest in the sky, with their eyes on the future. But, are our people living in their past glories or what? By this non-heroic child abuse in our lands, children are inimically disregarded in a generation that has abolished child punishment.

Children are scorned, cursed and easily insulted by parents and elders, as this is gradually becoming part of our culture. In many occasions, our elders act towards their children as if all the problems in our lands exist either because of the children or for their existence. These essentially useful blessings and rewards of marriage are unjustly treated without reciprocal respects, without love, and without assistance in their basic necessities in life. Hence, in numerous capacities, our elders are wrong in the government and its parastatals in the land. In the schools as teachers and Lecturers as well as parents and guardians at home and all other places of life where they are encountered often as people in control of affairs.

There are so many blames in life and these are channeled to the children and youth who are often innocent. It appears in Nigerian experience that there are holistic discomforts in the life style of the unassisted youth. These almost abandoned groups of humanity are in many occasions discouraged by attitudes of the leading group in schools and politics of the society that many are fed up with their existence while others are dying in silence. Many African children have no homes today those who are in schools are hungry. Perhaps nobody gives them hope for a useful future. All we meet is a wretched life, some in wretched begging attitude. Our streets are lacking care and generosity.

I have always seen in many villages how parents cursed and molested their children. I did see in my schools how older people mortgaged and easily infringed upon the rights of the youth. I have constantly come across in the streets numerous uneducated but easily marginalized and frustrated African youth, and many have gone mad as they lose hope considering the level of uncertainties that blur their future, as they roam about as sheep without a shepherd. So many cannot be sure that there will be a blessed tomorrow as the impressions they are given about today are quite annihilating and dehumanizing. Yet people who ought to be heroes are stealing away our Nations natural blessings in terms of money and wealth to those continents developed by their equals.

African Elders and Heroes

They have ruled our nations

They made us poorer than we were

They transported our fortunes

But left behind greater ill fortunes

None of them is patriotic

For that riches which did not

Reach home who gathered it?

None is wise for wise men will

Leave a place better than they found it.

Yet they are African Elders.....men!

Some of them aim to come back to power

But the youth of Africa! Will you be silent!

For evils to be done twice at home

Perhaps there will be rebellion in Africa

for elders to stop deceiving us!

Wise will be the children and the youth' who will not ignorantly go on to accumulate undeserved curses and unjust deprivations simply because their domineering opponents are elders. For evil respects not the doer.

Those done by our elders are still evil. As a child today can still be an elder tomorrow and evil today has a repercussion tomorrow.

Above all in line with the remarks of Bishop Desmond Tutu (1978:356) H.

The youths in Africa are given the ill answers to prayers they never said, and questions, they did not ask. He had maintained that "the African man was redeemed from sins he did not believe that he committed, and answers were given to questions he did not believe that he asked".

Now, imagine this odd experience of mine "Just for the first time in life, she saw me and she changed her mood to anger! I noticed all her feelings but I further discovered that the only problem is that I am younger and she was not happy being older, and seeing a happy youth". It seems they are seldom happy who wasted their own youthhood if they see others beautiful, optimistic and young'. When they meet the youth who are progressively aware of their youth hood. They may call them bad/ nicknames and even regard them as cowards. But why all these hatred in the soil of Africa? For no matter her feelings, I should not become a slave of those who wasted their own youth days in regrettable vanities!

Those who detest the sight of noble ambitious children who shared the innocence of nature unadulterated by another or evil. Is this not why the most high warns all people saying;

"Do not be ashamed to correct the old dotards

Who bickers with young people! Then you will

Show yourself really educated and win the

Approval of everyone" I

Yet in another portion he cautioned "Allow the little children to come to me, do not stop them. For it is to such as this that the kingdom of heaven belongs" J .

Now can all people not see that even the creator has constantly cautioned what this discuss is echoing now? Or does he not know all the ills that the youth' suffer in the hands of elders? We ought to be heroes. For even in the schools, if they failed you, you failed and if they pass you, you pass. Thus the success and failure of our youth depends holistically on the elders even as they abandon schools at the mercy of industrial actions.

In our families, villages and countries, they indoctrinate the youth with lesser love and bigger hatred. They deal with us violently than natural essence permit. They seldom teach the youth how to live without violence. For would that young ones learnt not violence at home.

In Africa, many are still bowed down in superstitious beliefs. As some of these are domineering determinants of decisions in the land. They seldom believe that knowledge can be innate in all humans' even children. Thus, they practice the same pennywise pounds foolish with which the Greek politicians misunderstood and abused Socrates the noble philosopher. Just prejudiced, they claimed he was corrupting the youth. Youth must therefore be allowed to learn from greater wisdom than culture. As certain cultures were ignorant coinages of people in their primitive times, often products of ancient ignorance.

Is it true that the future of a people is its youth? Hence, all leaders should learn to encourage and empower the young by appreciating their good ideas. No evil should be allowed to become prevalent in the countries no matter who does it, for in defecating all men go naked at least this makes all men equal. Developing the potentials of the young as instrument of solving lives' difficulties is our world's cyclic challenge. It is the way Africa can join the wider world to grow in integral civilization.

Heroes are those who can keep the flag of Justice Flying, patriotic citizens who let go their ego. They kept working and vindicated their people. Though many seem invisible today, in the time to come all will respect their existence. As they abolished evil, it is by their labours that heroes' wisdom, offered in their good wills becomes the wheels of human history.

They are not assassins of fellow humans Heroes are men of selfless Justice. Heroism fears nothing, as heroes do no evil. Genuine heroes sell themselves to buy others.

African Elders and Heroes

But some Africans believe that the greatest thief is the richest man.

Can a man hate his own fatherland and yet he struggles to be its leader, shall men qualify for wisdom if their only ambition is to grow richer than their country?, can anyone truly claim to be rich if his fellow countrymen whose resources he usurped are hungry and dying of poverty, ignored as victims of penury in a world where what matters is what you did to better the earth, what your contributed to help make the world a better place, not what you have stolen and deposited in foreign banks as most African politicians had been involved in.

C. H. Zudes

SIX | Double Standards

The expression of the term Double Standard can be understood as a verbal coinage, which describes the qualities lived out by people. This is an emphasis of a way of life people exhibit. As the diction stands, it implies a dual mode of living falsified life. The idea of "double standards" is a satirical approach to the life that is immodest and unworthy of emulation. It is another way of describing impostors, who live what they are not, by avoiding what they ought to be.

This is undeniable, as many people exist under this classification of human behaviour, among these can be found both the some youth and some elders alike. But it will become a rhetorical question, simply meant for emphasis if we spend time to ask, which group learns this from the other? We shall keep the same path of sincerity in consolidating the facts that this quality still exist in religious practices of the people. In their cultural exhibitions of their daily life and is ever dominant in the political landscape by which nations are governed by men.

It is a rampant phenomenon in human society; no sincere person admires it but many insincere people presume it as the right thing to think like this. But it is one of the foolish ways by which people desire to perpetuate their crimes of obnoxious selfishness as a life pattern, often influenced to be called culture.

As double ways or standards are never meant to constitute any reasonable feature in the life of man who is a young person. This is another type of illusion of life, by which some are afraid of being known as either good or bad. It is a way of thinking by which many others become pretenders. Infact, this is a symbolical representation of sycophantic behaviour.

We have spoken much about the three major divisions, of factors that give rise to the problems that devalue the underdeveloped African such as: Religion, Culture and Politics. In these, we did not spare the elders and leaders, but consistently and constructively criticized the wrongs which origin they constitute. However, one cannot avoid balancing this critical and analytical approach to them. We then look at the other side of the coin by appreciating another group of elders who are faithful, kind and worthy of emulation.

Following these condition above, we are here to discuss three prominent elders who proved themselves qualitative personalities and responsible leaders who count as representatives, symbolic images of all those who do not have the wrong notion of the destiny of the young.

In the religious perspective, I have to accord honour to Rt. Rev Dr. M. U. Eneje of Blessed memory, a retired Bishop of Enugu Catholic Diocese, Nigeria. Those who know him appreciate that he is a shepherd worthy of emulation. While many silently copy his footsteps, those who could not, take admiration in the direction his spiritual vision provided. He was in his life time, a strong embodiment of what a human spiritual leader should be.

As in his days, there was serenity, harmony and those who served God under him saw in him a great shepherd that would not lead them astray and one who led the sheep and ever ready to ensure they would not be scattered. He was never enslaved to material pursuit. I had the privilege to have known him from both long and short distance, in and out of leadership office, so, I feel personal about his virtuous life when compared to the days after him. Of him, one can appreciate that the positive spirituality of the old, elders and leaders would be contagious to the young, in this you see that simple life of holiness, without stress, of leading men and women in society is enough education to the young, as one elderly good man can disarm an army of irresponsible youth and his good examples would make them responsible.

Another instance is of cultural musicians, like the late Celestine Ukwu, who died in early 1980's and the 'Gentle-man' Michael Ejeagha a prominent one in local folk lore, music of enlightenment about the past history and a pragmatic direction for the future especially as it affects the young. All his music confirms the ethno and hallowed philosophy of life among the Igbo-African people often presented in local parables, others in fables, tales told in the names of unique animals. This also confirms the natural truth that humans are brothers and sisters of lower animals. Those who understand this today, keep animals as pets but many care for them more than their fellow humans. In him you learn of the mistakes of the anti-heroes in the human history, that even the elders and some ancestors are to be held blameworthy for some inappropriateness of human society today. It will tell you why life is how it is.

You will also learn about heroes and their roles to change the state of life for good in their days. Unfortunately our's pretend to be an un-learning generation. I have constantly seen people who make wrong allusions to such lucid contributions to enriching our world of knowledge. Some simply understand this great teacher of human history past, present and future as a mere story teller.

It is very painful in our world that our people water-down wisdom and positive philosophy for life meant for our sustainable and integral development, in this attitude of ridicule, some call it story-in-music, 'akuko n'egwu' thinking they are both long and useless, simply left out for casual entertainment. Jokingly, I hear people say; "akuko n' egwu Mich Ejeagha", whenever they do not cherish a story. No one seems to remember Celestine Ukwu whose music teach full details of various philosophies of life.

In this, we throw back this part of African wisdom for life of greatness to one man alone, because he courageously showed talent to develop our collective values left on the mud of forgetfulness. I have constantly seen in my works as a professional pragmatic Philosopher that; "in this part of the world, we waste values, belittle talents once it comes from another African.

We take nothing good serious, even those things destined to make us rich in the long-run. This is why Africa and Africans exhibit a poor outlook in life, and the world is ridding us because of this". This is not authentic Existence Africans! So, is this the life for any young person to emulate?

What then is a better fate you are herein challenged to create for your own generation as a promising African child? What name will you leave in history to be remembered for? Are you just there condemning the good works of others? It simply means you do not exist. You are a 'Da Sine' just being there!

For the young persons who cares to listen, this music for me, like many others contains serious secrets for life of greatness. This is one of the treasures that Africa has, and we are very busy wasting them. Would that I find time to translate them to foreign languages like French, Latin, German, Italian and English, people in Igbo land would discover that over the years, we have been sitting upon diamonds; still our continent exhibits colours of darkness in these blankets of poverty.

What exactly do we export to the world stage as African morality? Or is it enough act of existence for the giants in Africa to watch the naked- immoral vanities destroying the human dignity like homo-sexuality, Gay marriage and Lesbianism of Europe and America, without offering this world any reputable competitive moral alternative?

I consider it timid vegetative shadow of existence, for the African person, if he and she lives in a world, and simply feels comfortable accepting this ill-fate to be under influence from birth to death, without offering influential challenge to his/her world. If Europe and America evangelized and colonized Africa yesterday in its darkest hours, today, it points to the fact of moral darkness in Europe and America. The African destiny in us would be both latent and vegetative if we go on to sit on the fence, lacking in confidence and capacity to package those dignifying moral values of Africa as African Missionary journey/ package for Europe and America moral reconstruction.

If we cannot put on the candle of moral-life of authentic African people, we have failed as humans who came to birth in Africa. Our people lack wisdom, if they go on to contemplate today in some senate houses of adopting Gay-marriage and Lesbianism, as part of African custom, even the senseless animals we rear would consider this as foolishness.

In the study of philosophy of existentialism, no one exists, no one 'is' if he or she have no alternative, no right and ability to choose the good and reject what is not good in any society. If one has no freedom to say no to evil, such a one does not exist.

Truly, in Africa, be you youth, elder or even a leader, you have no claim to moral existence as you do not exist if you cannot stand by African morals, upholding this candle light of moral virtues often hidden in most cultural folk tales like music. There should be no contemplation of Lesbianism and even Gay marriage among African people. The youth should rise against this ill-fate.

With this, the young people of Africa can create a new world order, of progress through rekindling the moral dignity of man, exporting to the world stage, virtues of authentic African people to rekindle the somersaulting moral ethics of Europe and America. It is wrong for Africans to remain at the receiving end of almost every event in life.

It is therefore for the youth to evaluate their existence, from the perspective of what one can contribute to lives' stage, not just what you consumed from the stage of life, as has been common with most African societies, where neither serious invention nor major manufacturing takes place. "The black person in the views of Walter Rodney was actually, made a socio-economic and socio-political victim through the on-going dependency syndrome, in those silent politics of colonialism and imperialism that began in the early hours of the 15th century, leading to these economic humiliations meted out to Africans today.

"His local production sites were destroyed such that he and she would be restricted to importation of goods and services and that is one way Europe underdeveloped Africa" K.

Young people from African descent must therefore, wake up to the bitter-truths of human history and give up these penchant of affordable pretence, in which many of us contribute to making our black race look inferior to others. In this life, let us see it that what you contribute can make you great and what you consume can mar your greatness.

It is in our hands to help kick start the industrial age of Africa, which is one arm of age of pragmatism in our time. Only by so doing that you and I can achieve freedom in Africa and only this freedom can we offer our generation integral happiness and only this is the true essence of human life on earth.

No one is made great by copying or spreading evil, as most young people do

today not knowing that, evil ruins its doers, while

goodness is its own reward.

Good life and hard work can make a young person great tomorrow; it alone can make Africa and Africans great. Only the youth can do this, only the youth can still change the world. "Youth is an opportunity to do something and become somebody" L.

Finally in politics, Nze Stephen. N. Agu, a timely former Regent of Ngwo, all of Enugu State, in Eastern Nigeria. He is one of the few favoured politicians who was a onetime acclaimed best performed local government chairman, under whom, every town subject to his leadership seemed to have got some useful attention as the local level of funding could afford, yet he remained one of the very few politicians who did not fall into changing one car after another at the expense of the citizens welfare. In him can be found an admirable life of a good Educationist and economist.

As a politician, he proved a sensible model that young people in African can emulate without being led astray. He proved that corruption is neither a constant nor must it be a culture in the life of African politicians.

Also the fact that after being a Local Government Chairman, without coming out very rich, and a prominent town like Ngwo, made him the Regent to the throne of Ngwo clan, holding the people's crown until a new leader was to be chosen. It all shows that if you represent the human society very well without being corrupt and never losing your kit and kin, that the same human society will elevate you, giving you more honor and dignity that corrupt rich people would never have, inspite of all the money they have stolen, pretending to be very rich.

Being an educationist, haven been a great teacher for so many years, he further proved a great point and showed a sensible direction that every young person can afford to be a good leader in future politics, if they should first of all develop their area of life's profession and work hard in their given career. Truly, a creative person and all busy successful people in practical life, have 70% chance to avoid being corrupt in political position. But if out of indolence, laziness and act of having no employable career or business, any one pretends to claim to be a professional politician, such that whether in or out of political position. He or she hangs around politics in the empty theory of do or die game, such people, would be liabilities to human race, they have 89% chance to become corrupt leaders.

They cannot be considered as models and young people in any of the African nations, objective leaders should afford to create successful careers before entering politics, believing that good leaders can afford to do well in one tenure and give chance to others to make contribution, for only in this kind of decent thinking can we afford to achieve a peaceful progressive world in Africa, hence, offering a great model to the rest of the world's continents.

Double Standards

It would therefore, be double standard for the young people if they fail to look up to those elders who have similar character like the above three singled out, evaluated and discussed summarily.

Double standards are responsible for the setbacks and necessarily avoidable mistakes that befall our lives as a people of one continent. It includes all those attempts to steal money from leadership position, and launder them in more developed continents as most past pretentious leaders have done, given the Nigerian experience over the years. Yes, double standard because, they were called to serve and they left that mission and began to pursue shadows.

It is the same theory in the case of religion, faith and spiritual life, where among the preachers and leaders, many Christian teachers in religion know that fire is burning in their houses, they left it, went on busy in pursuit of the Rats in the bush. This happens each time they contradict the mission, that instead of directing people to and bringing glory to the name of the Almighty God, they make themselves the centre point. They create the place of worship as their family business often you will notice bill-boards showcasing husband and a must be fine looking-wife in the case of most Pentecostal churches. But was this what Jesus left as a standard?

If God Almighty is the one glorified, why do you project your own self images? For the same thing you oppose in orthodox churches like the Holy Roman Catholic, claiming they worship images that are truly divinized, like the Most Blessed Virgin Mary, is what you replicate in worshipping human images that are not even divine; neither do most of them ever give credence to holiness.

Therefore, is this not, both a double standard and a commonsensical fallacy? When today, those who frowned at the honor given to the Blessed Virgin Mary, Mother of Jesus Christ by the members of the Holy Roman Catholic church, are presently comfortable or pretending that there is no guilt/error committed when, their own Wife, Mother or even Sister is given similar honour as wife or mother of pastors. Can you not see now, some element of "Anti-Christ" in some of these pretentious churches? Since any form of disregard for the mother of Jesus Christ, is a visible characteristic of anti-Christ, as Christ never disregarded her.

For Christ insisted that there would be one flock and one shepherd. But many are led by ignorance or devil's pride and ungodly powers to divide the body of Christ, which is the Christian church. Dividing the body of Christ is Anti-Christ.

Jesus also insisted that those who do not gather with him scatters, so anyone who is of Jesus Christ, would not cause division or proliferation of churches, for

Jesus' mission was to gather together the scattered children of God.

Double Standards

Similar double standard life can be found among Moslems, they teach us to believe that Islam is a religion of peace, but my question is; how often are they the ones suing for peace in our world today? How often have members of the Christian sect shed the blood of Moslems? Compared to how many times Moslems have shed the blood of Christians given the endless holocaust of northern Nigerian experiences. This has become like an ancient ritual yet to be stopped, yet elders in these places of worship are keeping calm. The question is where is that peace? If they said they are a religion of peace.

For if we claim to love peace and within the slightest claim of provocation and even when there is non we rush to shed blood, ensnare lives and cause harm, distract the concentration of any government, in our search for a continued regional oligarchy of our own tribal interest. Do we forget that authorities come from God/Allah? If we oppose what God has instituted, how do we claim to be his children, followers of his prophet or people who serve God? Is this not lack of knowledge?

Are we not ruining the earth, if we are, is that not double standard?

We must embrace these truths and stop leading the youth astray if as elders people desire to have a happy old age. No one can eat his cake and have it. No great man sues for war in time of peace, the great are gifted to forgive, often those who lack greatness are seen trying to prove strength. For in the theory of Tigritude N a Tiger never says "I am a Tiger", no he merely demonstrates it. So if we say we are peaceful, or if any religious group lays claim to being the most peaceful in the world, let them demonstrate it, at least, by being the ones to offer other groups hands of peace.

Tolerance, is one of the first principles of wisdom, it is ignorance if people pretend that beyond what they believe there is no other religion, for a true worshiper of God/Allah , must go beyond these modes of worship mentioned above, like fighting , killing, maiming others, bombing the earth, thus furthering political frontiers in the name of any claims or belief of religion. So never ever think that beyond your own style of worship, no other should be allowed, this is not a way to develop Africa.

 For the true seed of development, germinates through cosmopolitan societies which means the meeting point of many-ethnic, multi-cultural and sophisticated societies, it was this kind of meeting together of slaves from different parts of Africa and other continents, during the slave trade that made the United States of America so great, so vast in scientific inventions and technology advancement.   China and India has also achieved this through freedom given to others to stay with them in their own land, without shading of blood in the name of defending any religion or its belief. Today, Canada is seeking the same by inviting career people with many skills into their land.

Double Standards

Nigeria like many African Nations has both by nature and even the gracious amalgamation of its protectorates in 1914 been entrusted with this, but out of ignorance, coming from various cultural myiopsm which stands for not knowing one's own limit, we fight wars, wasting precious opportunities and privileges destined for African greatness, indeed, ours is majorly, a double standard life so far.

In the views of Mr. Silver Ikowete; "Many African people live in darkness because of poor mentality, leading to low self esteem in modes of thinking of some apparent privileged ones, who return to the villages to play the local Rich-man mentality. These ungrateful sons and daughters of Africa, may be politicians and others manipulate the business system to accumulate more profit than they truly deserve, with these ill gotten wealthy man mentality, they come home to become obstacles to development of the home front, these are truly responsible for impoverishing the people from their own parts of the world".

"Imagine in a village, someone proclaims himself, a prominent politician, in the federal government level; he may have the status of a minister or such heavy-weight political influence. He treasures secretly to siphon any money budgeted to electrify his home village or demanding to use his secret company to collect the contract of constructing both high traffic and low traffic feeder roads of his home state, over the years, these roads are never built nor ever constructed. He siphons the money, keeping his rural community wretched".

He multiplies difficulty of his people and still parading himself as a leader of the people. How is this leadership? Is this what we consider as politics in our continent? If the youth revolts against these evils he proclaims them restive, criminals and anti-government or even Boko Haram. Who is a criminal and anti-government in this common example? This is widespread in Eastern and Western and South Southern and even northern Nigeria of our time.

Back home, he is the only one whose house has got electricity or mega generator that can afford to give light to an entire village, yet, this black person, gratuitously if not senselessly, is happy to be the only one whose house has light in the entire village.

But if anyone else out of sheer hard work and success dares to posses light in the same land, the double standard leader seeks to find out who exactly has done this, 'who dares me?' he thinks, he goes all out to hunt, crack down and maim the new fellow's progress, destroying his business and where possible, create circumstance to imprison him as a common criminal". This is another way many Africans are put in prison today, even when they are innocent.

This is the local mentality of success in our Africa, where fellow black men and women, keep the rest of their fellow Africans in darkness, in bad road, while the only good road is that street leading to their selfishly built houses".

Surely, this is not progress either to the individual or his local society and to our Africa. It is simply an act of cowardice, a sheer echo of brutish black capitalism in an age, where the only thing required of Africans like everyone else is black pragmatism, like upholding virtue and good life leading to internationalizing the African decent morality to help correct these stinking immodesty of Europe and America, which suggest new human naïve cultures like in lesbianism, Gay-marriage and sodomy. If we terminate this, we help make this world a better place.

American and European economies are surely getting bad because of the above dirty cultures they are promoting. China and India are taking the lead, since no one can oppose God or upturn the order in nature and remain on top. This is a lesson to China, India and Africans not to become seduced in these evils that have ensnared Europe and America of our time, but lend a helping hand to help deliver them back to moral pages of history.

This is a truth that takes only a philosophic ontological persuasion to point out, it also takes a philosophic mind, philosophic leadership vision from lovers of truth to understand and respect this attempt to correct things, thus put it into practice to be able to help make the world a better place.

C. H. Zudes

In the entire human world, of which Africa is part of its population and divisions, human beings are distinct from non-rational animals. As a cultural being, it is the cultural ability of man that makes adaptation possible for him in any environmental change or challenge of his. Therefore, apart from his reason, culture is another relevant aspect of life that stands to extensively distinguish man, in over -coming nature and influencing his environment for the better. Many look at culture as people's way of life. Others believe it is their ancestral heritage but some are too devoted to what they regard as culture. Hence, their culture can be the epitome and hallmark of their life on earth. Looking at various people and their various approaches to culture, one can conclusively distinguish culture in two dominant ways thus:

a.   The human inherited culture and The human achieved culture

Often the inherited culture is regarded as sacred and a non-violable phenomenon. It is normally built up and supported with folk tales as well as myths and legends. This aspect of culture may be either general or particular with different people and is seldom meaningful to other people outside those to which it belongs. In many observed and critical evaluations of it, it is often primitive, obsolete and upholds the cruel nature of man. It is subjective and upholds the divisions of mankind, especially on issues of racism, tribalism and cultism. As those outside these limitations, are seen as non initiates and inferior

Most of Africa and some myopic western people relate at this level.

The achieved cultures seem modern as they are products of intellectual efforts of man as "necessity is said to be the mother of invention". They give more credence to the rational nature of man. By this, humans use culture as a means of upgrading the standard of life in their existence. For by this, man does his reasonable best to make out the best in his creation. This has the quality of being easily loved and welcomed by all as any people can enjoy it and make it a new way of life better than the old. It shows objective nature of culture, especially the dynamic abilities of man as in inventive actions. It upholds the unity of mankind as in ideas of humanistic and utilitarian theories. More developed countries pay more attention to this kind of culture.

In Africa, many relate culture with religion hence so many cultural patterns of the people's life are inseparable from their religion. By this, their way of life cannot but be the religious way. In this context, not everybody can like this inter-mingling of religion and culture. This is why those who love it optimistically call Africans religious people. While those who dislike this, pessimistically call them primitive people or regard them as pagans.

These are variation in human perception and evaluation.

In achieved culture of the non-African or more civilized countries, people give greater credence to education, scientific mobilization of youths, in their talent harnessing and development leading to massive computerization of their homelands. While in the majority of the African countries, greater credence is given to factors of accusative value like ritual sacrifices, cultic initiations as in trends of and objects of entertainment such as masquerades, title-taking, dancing and feasting as is seen in numerous ceremonial activities.

Our people often have poor ideas about culture some love so much what they inherited in spite of the absurdities involved, these seldom reason beyond myopic limitations.

No wonder most of African seem to be back ward in civilization. Others seem to sleep still in the lumber-rooms of ignorance towards the much-needed challenges of growth, in scientific projections of our world today. Why are we so clouded with pessimistic superstitious beliefs? Many are still indoctrinated with blood conscious spirits of our dead fore-fathers, the good and bad alike: But at their departure, fore-fathers left greater sinister and superstitious beliefs as the major land marks for their descendants' inheritance. They existed with little wisdom and left behind them few fortunes. Why must our future lie on their limitations?

Even now, it is obvious that, if our ancestors return, to visit the living, in comparism with the few good legacies they left behind, they will prefer to flog a hell of senselessness out the heads of most of the leading people as well as those followers who play the sycophants, for failing to rise beyond those limitations they inherited, and not making effort to take the battle back to the white people, at least, colonizing them to buy into or at least respect the African morality, and values as another treasure the entire world needs now.

Africans need to influence nature with culture and not be influenced by nature as culture, for development, modernity and growth in science ought to be our way of life today. The more civilized worlds still know that man is a cultural being even in their nature of modern existence. Why must these-squalid adventures among grey hairs be accepted as our only basis of culture?

But why these monotony of indoctrination and deprivations? Our youths are hindered from attaining their fortunes. As our cordiality has given birth to no greater fortunes than futility. Why must Africans allow our distanced brethren to tantalize us with wisdom continuously?

Pathway of Knowledge and Culture

How we regard culture and what we regard as culture has deceived some people, ruined others and their inclinations has impoverished many humans, kept apart from reason and attempts of nascent science. It seems that while the other parts of the world are growing in science, Africans are growing in culture. Still many are prevented from seeing the mistakes of fore fathers, lest they grow in intelligence and understanding to correct it.

Shall we not weep for our soil, so concerned with ceremonies of blood and daily desire for dancing and drinking that has sapped some youthful intelligence? Minds are thus un-separated from emotional thoughts. Some people are debased and encapsulated with inclinations to initiation ceremonies in glorious thick forests at night, which has ruined intelligent strengths. Many youth have often been initiated into cruel occultism, societies often led by the elders.

Imagine this happening in our rural communities now, perhaps, in the name of braving up for winning political powers in the future, but power comes from God, and no one can bribe God to give him /her political power because he or she is an occult member. When even some people are given power by God and they become occult members and idol worshippers, these lead the society and the youth into evil and Godlessness. This kind of leader departs from humanity and behaves like a Animals, just like a Lion, Dog or Cat they feed on blood.

This is another reason for corruption, when the apparent leader is no longer behaving like a human being, this evil was common in the 'ancient' Bible history of people of Israel, but such evil leaders brought the anger and punishment of God on their entire family where often the prophet sent by God decrees and it comes to pass, the death of an entire family of such evil leaders as in the case of king Saul, king Ahab and Queen Jezebel and king Jeroboam.

What then is political power if after it you ruin your entire generation because you became devilish and Godless? Imagine King Nebuchadnezzar he lived in the bush and ate grass like Goats, Cows and Cattle for seven years before God restored him to human order. Every occultism in leadership is human disorder!

Such bad cultures are detrimental to the basic features and welfare of any youth.

Imagine this African true story and how a youth was easily misbalanced because of the affinity of elders to culture.

"It happened that this young man has been bereaved of both parents. Just like Naboth's Vineyard, they left for him a precious and spacious expanse of land. "An African local rich man came home and wanted to build his house. Traditionally he did his best to take away the boy's land but never succeeded.

Pathway of Knowledge and Culture

At last, he had to succeed by buying up the elders with wines and tobacco (utaba) and money. All the elders thus bought over conspired and claimed that this innocent youth is a thief and troublemaker. He had no option than to be arrested by the police, from police to prison, there he remained.

Consider then the Nigeria police, Army and other security forces as elders; are they source of security or agents as elders, of betrayal and insecurity in our lands? This is how many, good and innocent African children are languishing in the prisons even now, which has become their home unjustly. Is there any justice and peace in the hands of the respected elders in our countries and continent? Out of ignorance and cowardly fear, people fail to be just or correct injustices.

Modification is essential to all that nature has bestowed on us. A little wonder that only when you:

"Direct your thoughts,

Control your emotions and

You ordain your destiny". -Oliver Goldsmith.

Imagine also that some of the youth who thought fast have been ruined because of cultural bonds. Thanks to Mary Slessor's timely intervention if not, no family will have twin children today, including my family were my immediate elder brothers, are beloved twins of a world class delight. I would never have known them, just because of our empty claims of culture. Many and uncountable scientific minds from Africa have been slain; many were used to bury our perceived kings who died, others were poisoned in cultural festivities, not by anti cultural people but by the originators and fabricators of culture.

I remember a brief episode that took place in Abuja Nigeria, when that epic funeral ceremony of His Excellency, Chief Emeka Odumegwu Ojukwu was drawing near. I met a young lady and we became new friends, I mentioned that I was going to attend this expected epic funeral and burial. She simply exposed her fear that she would not attend because now that a hero is dead, they would use many human heads to bury him. I had known Ikemba somehow, so I told her that Ikemba is a good man and a Roman Catholic Christian also this is modern era. They would not use human head to bury our Ikemba, but she never agreed with me.

I had the opportunity to attend Ikemba's unique funeral and interment, and I carefully observed every event as many journalists did, with camera I had little or no restriction. So I had snapped every event that transpired.

I saw everything that took place to the point of lowering the hero's body to its final resting place and there was nothing like use of human body or human head to bury the greatest 'IGBO MAN' that lived especially in our time. I was happy to learn that my argument was right, and that Igbo people are capable of transforming such weak aspects of presumed cultures to more decent experiences as in this case of 2nd and 3rd February, 2012 of Ikemba's burial in Nnewi of Eastern Nigeria

No one denies that culture may at times be good and in other ones be bad. But we must think twice about our destiny and then re-position our culture. To be human, already is cultural only animals and plants can be natural beings. Then why these impositions of unscientific principles, many call evil culture?

No culture is divine, but whatever is divine is liberal. Why then must human desires, obstruct his neighbour's, leading them to greater hunger and insecurity? Imagine when few black people are well fed and fellow black men and women are hungry and starving. At this, always remember that whenever you ignore them, you are killing them. As they die, note that you cannot buy blood relations in any market in this world, not even in heaven. No one can buy the African Blackness in even the most expensive markets of this world. Be wise then and see with me why you must now stop all acts of war, all shedding of innocent blood and everything thing leading to the death of a follower African, either in the name of culture, politics or religion that you are in love with.

Sympathy to Culture:

In these attitudes of human preference to culture than greater values for life, to be philosophic enough let's inquire; what is the spiritual motivation or rational justification behind all these? Events in life have constantly revealed the origin of some of these unreasonable cultures. Yes our unskillful but culture custodians are too ready to carry on without due thought. They seldom reason before accepting.

Now, let us imagine the place of emotion and passion in developing our world? Often people in some African villages seem to be afraid to think correctly, yet they are suspicious of their children who care to think correctly. Sympathy to culture is any act of thinking that what is bad has become good, simply because it is part of culture.

As in the words of Munford Jones "Ours is an age which is proud of machines that think, but suspicious of humans who try to think".

The youth should influence their world, through their efforts, to accept the rational culture and reject showing sympathy to obsolete ones, it is sympathy to impure cultures that lead to sympathy for false national traits and ways of life which become cultures. This in itself is false nationalism, it is easily found in the way of life of most Nigerians. For it is not enough to be proud of what happens in other continents yet we remain suspicious of those who try to bring such great feats into happening in our own land and continents.

My place in African Beliefs:

An elder in one of the African nations accused the young

saying;

"I can justify that the youth have been destroying Nigeria since pre- independence" O.

But ours is not an age of parading blames, but the era of fixing our generation.

For we have been ruined by this sin of the ages, but why all these sins? As the Fathers have eaten the sour grape ignorantly and set the teeth of children on the edge. Like Adam and Eve they have achieved a predestined sorrow for their yet to be born children. I have always seen and experienced the depth of sorrow, which innocent children feel about the obsolete standards of cultural exhibitions in human existence.

Children, youth and a group of woman are suffering beyond the level of nature's recommendation. I disagree with ancient theories, beliefs and ideologies that worsen life for the African child. Who will believe that children are not born to suffer from the cradle of birth except the few people who are not too African in ideology? Our people have fashioned little or no right of fundamental happiness or even fundamental exercise of useful freedom to its younger people. They anchor everything to tradition and when a group of elders want to perpetuate a particular evil, they term it culture. Under the disguise of traditionalism, many obsolete principles have continued to poison our people's readiness to develop.

May we think about what the position of a learned person must be, what he should do. Is it to continue bowing to evils or to steadily oppose wrongs and give credence to virtues? I believe it is a time to uphold only pragmatic cultures, being the ones that solve the people's problems and offer them best results in given circumstances.

I love the position of a legal hero in Africa, the youths should learn from the late legal hero Gani Fawehimi of Lagos in Nigeria, when he said;

"I am self critical, re-examines and ever critical of myself"... He said more: "I will never give respect to any Traditional Ruler, in this traditional cue up, I am disappointed, and some are not traditional rulers but traditional Gamblers". They must be careful before they vanish from the scheme of things" P.

As a philosopher, what this legal giant of Blessed memory is actually saying is that most traditional rulers are poor because they left no youthful legacies like, Agricultural plantations, investments in Business and manufacturing industries, indeed they were never professionals in any reliable business of human dependence, when they were young. Now they are old, many are even polygamous with large families. Hence to survive, they depend on the politicians in government positions and other corrupt rich Africans, consequently, they cannot oppose any evil in society as elders, since they receive gifts that ensnares them into corruption.

This account for why no elders are available to play the roles of African elder states man to solve the real problems of our time.

This goes to justify as very correct, the noble words of President Goodluck Ebele Jonathan of Nigeria in his funeral oration at the hallowed funeral of the Noble Nelson Mandela, former trust worthy President and one elder statesman of his country, the South Africa at his death in 2013. But in local arrogance, many proud elders got angry and misunderstood President G.E. Jonathan's argument that: "There is no Strong Politician in Nigeria (Africa)". His view is correct and contemporary still challenging everyone, as there are no strong moral characters acting courageously to defend virtues here virtues are in exile.

My argument here will exempt very few Traditional Rulers like H.R.H Igwe I.O.U Ayalogu who invested greatly in agriculture in his youth, in recent history, besides massive employment to the youths and fellow elders, he is known to support politicians, contrary to those who depend on them, he helps them succeed, such a man is a model to African Youths as you will read further on him in the next few chapters.

This simply implies that any leader whosoever, will deserve respect when they uphold what is right in the land, but looses any merit of claiming to deserve respect when they soil their own hands with evil practices. All men are by their (second) nature cultural. Africanism is

C. H. Zudes

too natural to keep on submerging the essence of exhibition of our youthful potentials, with which African youth are endowed. Indeed, no good culture will hinder human advancement in civilization.

Pathway of Knowledge and Culture

EIGHT | True Freedom

The ideal freedom is an important factor in the life of every human person. It is an honorable right which man regards as one of the fundamental endowments by nature upon him. This is a very important phenomenon in the very nature and cultural advancement of man. Silently or laudably, every creature yearns for freedom.

Therefore true freedom is the deepest search of humans in this exercise for their liberal existence. This is the realization of man's ability to choose, reject or select his choice of freedom, which alone incites man to his greatest search and need in the world, which is happiness. As only, a free person can possibly attain a life of happiness.   Yes,   only   when   you   have   an alternative.

Some great philosophers have taken time to examine the concept of freedom. For them freedom is one of the basic sine qua non (you cannot do without) in the existence of all who actually constitute the numerical strength of human beings in the world. In accordance with Hegel, a freedom philosopher;

"The best freedom is freedom under law". This goes to indicate that human freedom have to be structured to fit into the reasonable scope of a given law in order to become a meaningful freedom. Therefore a true freedom can be seen in the light of "the best freedom "which must be under a good law. It therefore goes to substantiate that an unmediated freedom, not modulated by law, a careless freedom that leads to corruption like embezzlement, by political office holders, cannot qualify as a true freedom.

Jean Jacques Rousseau the philosopher: States that;

"Man is free yet everywhere in chains". For him,

man seems to be free, thinking that he is free but still wants to be free.

Yet in all that man regards as his freedom, he is still in chains at all times. This may go a long way in justifying the classical statement, that;

"where ones freedom stops, there another's freedom starts".

We must then examine the question. CAN MAN ACTUALLY BE FREE? Indeed, man can be free, but to be truly free. (As to enjoy his existence in true freedom) man must control freedom with reason.

Consequently, a true freedom is a reasonable freedom.

We must from this infer that if a man refuses to reason properly, he has equally refused to enjoy his freedom. For any action performed, which is not guided by adequate rationalism, (pure reasoning), subjects man still within the shekels of the chain, stopping his own freedom.

True Freedom

Then can the youth be free? The answer is yes but whether they are actually free or given freedom, is a subjective issue dependent on two categories:

(a) Dependence on the societies evaluation of freedom and

(b) Dependence on each individual's perception of freedom.

Considering a religious perspective the law of karma indicates that; "every action has a repercussion, every evil is punishable with another evil and that goodness is its own reward". These mean that if one chooses to do evil, one has chosen to do evil. Also as there is no rest for the wicked man, no man who acts wickedly aims at freedom, or good end. So, if the youth desire to be free and intends to enjoy (all) the basic fundamental freedom of a human person, the youth should avoid evil and do well, at least to achieve happiness, as one is rewarded only in goodness. In line with the above, for the youth to achieve true freedom in their lives they must begin by avoiding all kinds of evil, like corruption which implies being sinless. But "How can the young be sinless?" Q is the pragmatic question of the holy literature, the answer came? "By obeying your word (law of God)".

Consequently, this stands to justify Hegel's position of true freedom as above. It is then simple for all human understanding that a youth or anyone who sins has proved oneself unworthy of true freedom. Do you know that prisoners can be freer than those who imprisoned them?

Yes, if the prisoners are innocent and pure in mind. For true freedom is a matter of a spiritual value (the conscience) not of the physical/bodily. There are other conventional expressions, which holds that: "Freedom corrupts but absolute freedom corrupts absolutely"- (Anon).

And this is true. In every event in which humans are guilty of corruption and powerful agents of wickedness, it is basically because they have absolute freedom, without checks and balances of power, thus easily abused; consider the military anarchy and dictatorship in government, the embezzlement in public offices, it is this so called political immunity that generates this carnage culture, 'corruption'.

We must now discover why true freedom cannot be absolute as absolute freedom is not necessary for man, if he must be happy. A happy person is one who reasons properly, allowing reason to control his freedom, such must avoid selfishness. The youth should aim to obey God's laws; the good societal laws and the laws of genuine love, and prudently oppose the bad laws of any culture or society for only the opposition to evil laws brings true freedom, which in itself help man to achieve happiness.

NINE | Religion and Character

Religion is a great useful value for all people. It stands as that which man in conscience is bound to take seriously. As it is often a reference to worship by man in relationship to his God. By ways of its etymology: Religion came from the Latin word "Religiare" meaning to worship. In the views of Cicero; it means; "worship or reverential signs of divine worship and communication with the Divine".

Also "It is a relationship between humans and the super sacred" and Lacathantus holds the opinion that it is "human piety turned to the objective one, the divine person of which it is an obligation for man to fulfill". It is then a system of spiritual value, which anchors man to what he believes as his originator or the most powerful principle of his existence. As all men generally believe in things, it suffices to say that human beliefs can hardly be the same. Even God wants people to be different as in the era tower of Babel....

Religion varies as human life and opinions of essence of existence vary. In Africa certain people have religion not quite distinct from their culture hence, as the people's way of life is their culture; many African's have religion as the second nature of their way of life. Religion like culture is what holds Africans together. About religion in our lands these facts remain true that: some religions were imported and others were inherited.

Chinua Achebe the noble author of Things fall Apart opined that: "They have put a knife in what held us together and we have fallen apart". It may be this fall into corruption. That is the nature of the inherited African traditional religion (A.T.R.). This falling apart is the greatest challenge devouring the Christendom today, the human ego (the self), has come upon the ought to be Christian love of the earliest Christians. So many divisibility exist today in the things of God simply because of selfishness of many who pretend to be leading the faith, in a world where those who worship the devil as in the occult are so united as their only means to achieve progress, when Christians fail because they are deeply divided.

THE CONCEPT OF CHARACTER:

This tends to consider the moral strength and integrity of the people who uphold these varied natures of religion. It equally evaluates the good or bad reputation as official position of the leading men and women in these religions in their relationship with the human society as a family. Herein, Character may also connote the capacity of man in his response as a means of accomplishing his duties. Therefore, it is this character of man's that is the major influence on religion. And it seems that without this character, religion will not exist rightly. We must then evaluate religion and its moral strength and capacity in its influence on man.

Considering the second type of religion, the imposed religion is composed of the orthodox Christianity and Islam as well as any other minor sect that may still find its way into Africa. As in its gradual process of civilization, Africans have given greater credence to these imported systems of worship, having been influenced by its agents of: civilization and colonization. But how have our people adapted?

Going by the Christian faith, religion has been conventionally symbolized in the term "church", a congregation of people or children of God. According to Averry Dulles a Liturgist that is a scholar on modes of public worship, he described the church as;

> "A hospital where the children of God are treated,
>
> A refectory where they are fed and
>
> A school where they are educated".

It seems that the worshippers have infinite numerical strength. But unlike the African traditional religion and Islamic religion, Christianity, is a victim of an unrestricted nature of intensive disintegration and diversification, thus it is good to account for an unhealthy mode of religious proliferation in the Christian sect. This kind of undue proliferation in religion seems to be a way of its destruction seeing that the holy scriptures insists that Jesus prayed that they may be one and died to gather together the Scattered children of God. But certain Christians are busy thinking that what makes them godly is the echo of beginning a new church, this is one act of putting asunder to what God has joined together, it is a way of dividing the body of Christ, often leading the uninformed youth astray.

Imagine this story, an event of 2011 AD, of a young lady due for marriage after university education. She was turning down her potential suitor ready to marry her… when I inquired from her, since this dramatic episode was drawn to my attention, she opened up that she wants to marry a pastor to be, someone she can team up with to form a new church in the near future.

Then I asked her; do you know what is called polytheism?

She said no,

Do you know what is fanaticism or anthropomorphism?

She said no,

Do you know what proliferation of religion is?

She said no.

I said further, "What then do you know about religion for you to be starting a new church?"

This is a clear image of how love of materialism influenced by our not knowing God and ignorance of facts about religion is allowed to destroy the mission of our faith, that is another act of capitalism of religion and an abuse of man's co-creative potential as endowed on him by God.

But one may still patiently be tolerant of these modes of religious advancement for one simple reason, that: God is too holy, too transcendent to be worshipped only through one religious background.

Yet it is very wrong for anyone to think that what makes his own religion valid is the destructive criticism he can readily give to others in the progressive future.

Unity and Love are unavoidable challenges to all these multiplicity of religion. If its values will remain essential to man's need. Jesus prayed for unity of churches not for proliferation as many rush into today, replacing the call for spirituality and holiness of life with echoes of religiousness of mentality.

Following the recent trend of events in the entire human society, it seems that there is both fabrication and falsification of churches. In his book The Divine Deceit Fidelis. K. Obiorah outlines a roll call of more than 830 churches in Nigeria alone as at the year 2002 AD. Today, ten years later, imagine the yearly volume of divisibility leading to proliferation, leading the youth into the crisis of polytheism that must now have taken place and still repeating itself.

For him, it is the bad omen of "apostasy in the latter days, gradually being fulfilled as the Devil, like a chameleon has concealed his venom of wicked serpent in proliferation of churches, "where wicked deception in counterfeit miracles, will make many to believe what is false and taking pleasure in wickedness, would perish." R

He quotes Thomas Merton: who looks at indecent breeding of churches that:

> "It is a religion less, Religion!
>
> Nothing but man's wishes for himself
>
> Claims to preach, but toys with the truth!

Pseudo religion is far more foolish and superstitions". (Page 21-34).

Our major concern is that the young are still the greatest victims of these nonchalant abuses of religion in our time, as they love and live the attitude of Polytheism. Then, what is Polytheism; poly implies many while theism is from 'theos' the Greek name for God. Hence it points to many curious ways the youth perceive, love and choose to worship God, ie "worship of many gods, departing from one original belief to a secondary, a new way of worship".

Religion and Character

The nature of young people is this curiosity of life style which makes them not satistified with what they know, see or were taught but loves to make their own mistakes, often finding what is not existing, in a wandering curiosity, some claim seeing the light, yet not knowing they were never in darkness before.

They seek for new ways, fashionable alternatives and often tend to be inventive as a life style. These features are active in why proliferation finds common place among the youth, more of young ones are victims and very few elders especially unprincipled women fall victims too. And religious capitalists take undue advantage of this, pretending to be Preachers, Prophets and Pastors.

While leading men of orthodox religions like the Holy Roman Catholic Church are also guilty in this, when they take decisions, not minding if it plunges the youth into crisis, without plotting any handy alternative for them. Often they send the youth away from the seminary, for some they recommend their withdrawal, leaving them no sense of direction, not caring about even the 'faith' of these little ones.

Imagine this story which is a microscorm of many others, "I know a young fellow, who was my teacher, intelligent, morally ebullient and an excellent footballer, that besides the concealment of religion, of him, if he took football as a career, the world class renowned J.J. Okocha would not be better than him in dribbling an opponent in football pitch. His name is Jude Eze. We called him Shekibe, especially for his perfect dribbling in football. He was a reliable teacher of physical and health education. He loved to help people.

After so many years of education in a given field of endavours all we later heard of him was that he was sick (a certain yellowing of his eyes), that the colour of his eye was not acceptable to the religious authority and he will not be ordained a priest.

He was to be sent away, but who has shown him where to start life again?

From some where to nowhere? "Yes from a given direction to the confusion of facing an uncertain world. No one considered the sacrifices of the African youth over many years, upon all his childhood sacrifices, in the name of faith and religion, he has to lose everything, at this, what sets in is youthful crisis.

Tell me where Shekibe is today, in his prime of youth, he has joined the ancestors. He did not survive this crisis, frustration and confusion. He could not face the world again of beginning from no-where, as friends, admirers, the church and the family, would certainly ridicule him, with claims of sin he may not have even attempted to commit. "Yes, often people open their mouth to speak and scorn others, just because, they want to stop it from smelling". A noisy girl once taught me.

Religion and Character

He died, just like that! A talent, a youth and a silent hero was lost. The only reward he got was to be abandoned in such a time of crisis.

There so many like that especially from Nsukka, Enugu and Abakiliki Dioceses, where no one was found bold enough to oppose these evils of injustice and lack of respect on the rights of the youth, given the events of year 1999 AD.

However, my very Reverend Editor insists that there are so many who were sent away like that, and they make it up in life, he asks me what about them?

Yes, my very humble response is, "this is true, but do you know what you have put them to go through?

That many of them have gone though excruciating and devastating humiliations in life that when they ask themselves, what crime have they committed? What echoes back to them is; "you came to serve God, you answered his call in your youth."

 This seems like an invitation to make such young person to hate God and even the Church since, Their present life is not cheaper than burning through the imagined fire experience of hell, and of coming back to life from hell, from the world of the dead. Speaking from personal experience, the world they live in had already destroyed them they are here simply because they refused to die young. They looked up to believe in a superior destiny to what they have now lost.

Also, taken that this may be the new direction to their newer destiny, but how it was carried out and the style of this re-direction determines so much about the entire future life of the individual, this apparent prevailing crisis inherent in progressive advancement of some young people certainly affect our world, bringing ruin to a generation, a setback to black Africa, since it is not so in Europe and cannot be the same attitude to youth vocation for religious life in America. Consequently, every-energy in our generation should be employed to oppose such abuse of the young people's life as in the year mentioned above from happening to the youth in Africa again.

It was a year, when so many of the youth were flushed out of the seminary, may be because Africa have got enough harvest of the young people's vocation, more than it ever needed in this. Their story which was turned into a crime, they committed was; "you did not pass all your subjects and the Rector recommended that you be withdrawn". Conclusively, "you have no vocation".

Now, about twelve years after, I make bold to ask today, "In an imperfect system, in an imperfect world like ours, where a lecturer who does not like how you ask questions or the splendour of your face, decides to mark you down, is it enough to conclude that you have no requisite intelligence or vocation for a career?

One crime here is treating the youth like nobodies, perhaps because they are young, forcing them into frustration, to face a dark despairing world of confusion without any touch light for direction. It is not enough to conclude that a youth have no particular vocation. It ought to be the duty of the Shepherd, to involve professionals to go extra miles to understudy what psychological burdens the youth may be carrying undisclosed, or even unknown to him perhaps from the family challenges, help them to lighten it. As in, if they are not good in this, be particular in pointing direction to what and where they are good in, and how best to redirect them, simply because you have understudied them. But this was never done but youths were summarily dismissed.

The mother- church owes a lot to help rehabilitate them, not to treat them like out casts. After all, there are still the worst of it in the best of us and the best of it in the worst of us, as numerous latent talents lie undiscovered, so may be the real vocation of a youth.

Youth is an age of taking decisions and seminary from the Latin word Seminarium, means a seed bed, where people like plants are nurtured, helped to take the right decision of where to be transplanted to. It must not be a push pointer to the priesthood as many in society ignorantly claim and dangerously abuse the essence of human life; as families, friends and admirers disdainfully treat one who leaves the seminary as an out-cast in the society.

For me and many others, leaving the Seminary is

nothing different from that episode of life, when King David, in his youth, left Shepherding the Sheep(flock) of his father Jesse, at the custody of someone else, based on a secret instruction of his father, for an unknown higher assignment secretly kept for him by God. It was simply because he even left the Shepherd's work that was popular at that time in history, for an unpopular act, in this act of obeying the last order, known to him alone that he found himself where he was to take up the challenge on behalf of everyone else, in the whole land of Israel and he killed Goliath, who even those who presumed to be the chosen soldiers could not attempt to fight against. So, being among those chosen by God is not even the issue.

Consider how the enigma and ironies of life works in the silent obedience to these unpopular will of God. David at the battle field was that anointed 'Sacred Stone', rejected by the builders. But all these did not stop David from becoming the next king of Israel and now the greatest in records of history.

But in our own time, many people rush to ridicule those who must not become priests in terms like 'ex-Seminarian', forgetting that even the Priest and Bishops are all ex-Seminarians!

The term 'ex' simply means out of. And whosoever is no -longer in it, is out of it.

Therefore, it cannot under any sound logic be a term for

the select few you desire to ridicule, if that ridicule were to be a way of attaining Christian perfection, which alone is the ought to be target of every Christian life.

"Yes we make the youthful affliction of these youths more dangerous and disdainful than the affliction Job of the holy bible endured in the hands of God. Truly, because Job had at least three faithful friends like; Eli`phaz the Te`manite, Zophar the Na`amathite and Bildad the Shuhite and a wife, they played roles that also cooperated in making Job, in the end of his crisis (suggested by the Almighty God) recover double fold of things he lost". T

So what happens in our Africa, if a young man or woman loses a vocation to religious life, even if triggered up by God to see the strength of the individual's faith. Are you going to be among those who take delight in afflicting someone whom God is simply chastising to his own glory? God can send one to this exile. How exactly is that your business, leading to you scorning these whom you know little or nothing about their future destiny and has been redirected by God?

But today, in Africa, when a youth suffer an affliction in the hands of religious authorities, what happens from fellow Christians? You double their affliction by ostracizing and sacrificing them to the mockery of the world, deserted by friends, hated and relegated in the family, even in most churches, villages and towns. They are faced with losing any chance of getting help as humans.

In all these, we destroy our world, divide our faith, we play God in passing judgment and failing to even offer love, this love is the only one mandate and business of Christianity, but is this how to show love, by not helping the helpless youth because society or religion has hurt them?

"Those who have not seen life are so judgmental". No one knows or can say exactly why things happen as they happen. This life is an enigma, a mystery. Those who emphasize the apparent down fall of others as above, must dare to learn that; "the tragedy of life is not that you did not reach your group's goal, no it is in having no personal goal to reach which is different from everyone's. It is not in the not achieving the set target with your school mates, but in never having a private target in life to separate you from the crowd of men or priests". So learn to stop treating every exit as a tragic episode.

No one can say from where cometh the new Constantine. The old Constantine who was a pagan king/ Emperor but was never counted in the Christian faith yet, he was the one who decreed freedom to Christian's worship beyond the Catacomb where they used to hide to worship before the years around 325A.D.

Because of persecution in those days, today Christians are even used as present day persecutors of fellow

Christians. That is a pretense in our religious civilization, where those who presume to have succeeded in this or that....,

are seen to look down on those who appear to have fallen. But this human life is an undeniable enigma, for often, these tables of life's stage turn twice.

Who will legislate another / modern freedom for Christendom? Who will be the next Emperor Constantine of our time? Given the modern day crisis like Boko Haram, in Islamic Slaughter of Christians and religious riots, a funny culture in northern Nigeria, is another way of persecution and over decade's religious and political elders failed to stop this evil inferno. Even you Christians in politics!

Still some religious authorities are more busy, very busy with this echo of capitalism in our faith, of pretending that you are better than others, being 'the chosen and they the rejected', calling yours 'the living Church', implying others are dead churches, yours the bible believing church, and others what? But is that what you learnt from Jesus? If Jesus were to be here today, will he speak like that? It is those who have not seen life that rush to become judgmental.

Collectively, we have failed to correct the evil furnace and phenomenal that confronts the whole church. We make due with claims of who is the richest preacher, what a myopic materialistic mentality in Christendom.

If the church elders fail to correct these, they will be logically guilty of contributing in expanding the frontiers of confusing the youth, adding problems to the foundations of the weak old world which religion tends to play an act in healing with one hand, and with another hand inflicting this same injurious wounds.

This is because, some mono-linear minded youths not exposed to dynamics of religion, when treated like Shekibe above, when they are alive and could not restrain their curiosity for God, in the fantasy of their imagined spiritual gifts and presumed devotion to God, they end up fighting back by starting their own church. This is a silent reason for sporadic proliferation of churches today.

That is the business of Protestantism and anti-clericalism, and the clerics unknowingly instill this in the young, the less mature minds adapt to these.

This is one angle, where the authorities of the Holy Roman Catholic church is blameworthy in the on-going proliferation of churches, a wonderful capitalism in Christianity, simply because, it is often about who heads certain claims of religion and who propands the latest, scintillating slogans of worship.

I am bound in conscience, to pay tribute to His Grace, Rtd. Archbishop of Onitsha, Albert K. Obiefuna of blessed memory and Bishop Simon Okafor of Awka Dioceses, who in the event of year 1999 A.D refused to let their young seminarians be treated with those scornful abuse imposed on young people's life. For they resisted the Seminary authority's judgmental conclusions and sent their wards back to the school insisting that they were there for the school authorities to shape them into better people, but when it became politicized and capitalism played on, they still cared for their youth, sent to them to Ss. Peter and Paul Bodija, a seminary in Ibadan western Nigeria. Many of those written off that year as having no vocation to the priesthood are priests today, implying

that the initial judgmental withdrawal imposed in 1999 to many others who found no defenders, must have been faulty.

In his views, based on personal experience of the Author, he believes he owes a lot appreciation to His Eminence, John Cardinal Onaiyekan and Bishop William Avenya of Oturkpo Diocese. For the youthful crisis which came to many in such a year like 1999 could follow these young people if not all their life, to some for many years after it began, as they lose friends and everything they ever worked for. He observed that he only found solace and direction, away from this youthful crisis, in the year 2006 when he officially came in contact with the two leaders, especially John Cardinal Onaiyekan, the Roman Catholic Archbishop of Abuja, whom for so many years, the religious authorities in Enugu refused to give the author a letter to meet him with.

151

C. H. Zudes

It was him who after discovering some ideas of interest while hearing the author speak in defence of philosophy in a meeting of which also present, was Lady Shirley Ezenwanne, on behalf of other philosophers in the land. The religious leader offered him a hand of fellowship to become his Seminarian. In that same interaction in the Archbishop's house, the host was right in acknowledging that the absence of harmony in the family can lead the young people to perform less intelligently in schools and also lead to any kind of vocational crisis.

The experience spanned through a nine years exposure through the religious based education, which abruptly ended after the Rector of the Pope John Paul Seminary Awka, in whose office the author, worked in his daily morning function, who prior to this abrupt imposition of confusion, was a direct beneficially of the author's literary creativity especially in 'epic eulogy, presented in his honour 'as it got a universally applauded ovation, when delivered in Nnewi in during the 25th priestly anniversary of the Rector, and many other bright literary contributions in school of those era.

The irony of life here is that, after all they know, saw and observed that 'we' consist of, he signed 'us' off in a document that gave the impression that 'we' consist of neither virtue nor intelligence. This misrepresentation of facts about young people is a costly abuse of position of leadership and a youth's life. This is justifiable cause of confusion in the life of the young, for if they have discerned and directed properly, they would use their leadership capacity to show direction.

But it was not so, since it took an era of 1999 to late 2008 to arrive at a simple fact; "you have a talent for a career in literary works, spend your time to develop it". But this was never suggested, hence, all else was a ruining lie.

For example this episode of (wasted) years, gave rise to endless uncertainty, shadow pursuits and illusions just to find direction, simply because those who saw it as elders and 'leaders' hid it from the 'young'.

The climax of this search for direction was thus; "by end of 1999, I had been trying to discern my future; we used to be close to many priests, especially Rev. Fr. Camillus Ejike Mbaka, who along side Rev. Fr. Paul Ekowa at the inception of the new millennium, year 2000, when I confidently put aside the religious Garment "the Soutan".

They paid for my diploma in computer education in Enugu, when this was over, I was in touch with Very Rev. Fr. Prof. Obiorah Ike, who linked me to the promise of Scholarship in Madonna University Okija, as I planned to study law with it, thus he sent me to meet Very Rev Fr. Prof. Emmanuel Edeh, whom I learnt as he is called 'the Father founder', he also found me interesting to keep close by and directed me to go on and study law and access the assigned scholarship for Enugu Catholic Diocese.

However, this could not be because the conventional influence of African families on their youth separated me again from all these promising great friends, as from my family, an instruction came that I should simply go for a Federal university, it ended up to be Nnamdi Azikiwe University Awka.

Through the other youths who suffered the same crisis of uncertainty, I too, got to know the now Rev. Fr. Dr. Bonachristus Umeogu and Prof. Ike H. Odimegwu, Prof Godalex Ezeani and Dr. Paul Ogugua etc, all Philosophy lecturers, who as a team understood us. They linked us to admission in Nnamdi Azikiwe University Awka. It was now, in finding peace and promising academic stability in Unizik, was how and where this talent to write began to show fully, as I commenced and did 70% construction of this book in years 2001-2002, later on in searching for a moderator to my written works was what fetched for me the friendship of Dr. Bonachristus, who also saw in me great intelligence that must be encouraged, as he began to trust me with many treasures, dear to him, then he became Head of Department, till we graduated in 2004.

At home leisure hours, at home parish I taught Block Rosary children in the holy Rosary in French, Latin, English and German. Upon graduation, I had to teach Literature and Agric Science respectively but briefly in Nsude Seminary again after I did apostolic year there in 1996/97, and at Our Lord's Secondary School, Ninth Miles, before leaving home for researching the wider world.

Leaving home for the youth service in 2004, the future was still without direction as there was no body to point it, especially confusing because one felt he didn't have to look at these vicissitudes and abandon what appeared like destiny has assigned him;"the Priesthood". I had prayed to God to show me in which city my future lay by the outcome of my posting, as in if posted to the west, let it mean, my future is in Lagos, if posted to the north, let it mean my future would be in Abuja. Later, I was posted to the north.

During those days in 2004-2005 in Nasarawa State, I had to meet the Bishop of Lafia in Search of my vocation, 'but my vocation was not there', I was about three time in Niger state meeting with Catholic Bishop of Minna in search of my vocation, 'but my vocation was not there'. I had left Nasarawa to Enugu Diocese about five times to collect a letter in years 2004- 2005, for the religious authority in Abuja.

This was all these while refused me. I therefore took my irrevocable decision that after my youth service, if I spent 2 years in Nigeria without getting the admission overseas for it, I will abandon it as long I detested making a further approach to it in Nigeria, which may be why I kept silent when the unexpected offer came on a platter of gold from the Cardinal Onaiyekan . But shortly before this, I had prayed for a direction before meeting the now Bishop of Oturkpo who I had more closely been known to and he advised me to give up on it as; 'Everybody can not be a priest' which is fine.

Those Episodes of 2006 came to pass. In 2007 I had first hand impression of young people being abused in corporate but naked capitalism as I worked in Ecobank Nigeria Plc , which ended up paying some of us, university graduates only N15,000:00 in the name of contract work, it was an abuse of corporate ethics in Nigeria and African youths in Africa, but there seemed to be no moral authorities who could offer jurisprudence to repeal such negative laws, in this, the institution was corrupting the individual as this amount was too poor not create corruption for the individual whom it pushes into indebtedness, as in you must spend much more than you were paid just to go and come from work and get customers to the bank with same meager sum, of which I brought in over 200 customers and many with good business for the bank in less than one year. I had been waiting for the Fidelity Bank Plc's promise to invite me for employment interview after passing initial exams, but for so long and even for ever, this employment interview never came to be.

By 2008, I worked in a micro finance bank where, I met some quality authorities who became great characters for rebuilding youths, in some like Mr. Henry Nwawuba in whom I found compassionate leadership which offered attractive promises for your hard work. But as at then, many of the prominent business friends and customers I have known, would not accept to bank their money in a microfinance bank, due to uncertainties and preferences for mega banks. This became one reason why I must give up the work, since their mindset was outside this microfinance-banking and all we needed was to get them to bank in it, yet in about four months, I had over 100 customers brought in. This was a little better more friendly than the other banks.

I never got any free money because I worked for any bank. However, my silent growth in literary vocation, which was at then silently developing with four potential books quietly underway, came to lime light for me, when in pushing   signing on, the Federal Ministry of Works and Housing account, which the Minister refused to give attention to the Micro- Finance bank as obtained in those days. Pushing through the family and getting no head way. To avoid missing out all the way, 'I had to talk about my writing a book', and the wife of the Minister who felt happy to encourage young people was the first to show great consideration about this skill. She gave me some enveloped money; this taught me that instead of the unfair experiences going on as a banker, I can also succeed in this writing career which has at this moment become very evident in me. She is indeed my earliest superior direction pointer in life, funder and supporter and then, the genius in Engr. Sir. Emmanuel Mbaka showed me a more strengthened direction and part sponsorship.

I was further privileged to find favour with other great men of Roman Catholic Church like Chief Sir. Dr.

Emeka Okonkwo and Hon. Engr. Mark Uchendu, who at various times between 2008 and 2009 employed me with brotherly concerns to work in their business establishments where I worked briefly before focusing on this act of writing and like them, I met other favours of Talent funding from His Excellency, Chief Dr. Orji Uzor Kalu. These helps beside my family's support have kept my hard earned literary career on going; today it becomes avenues for some young people's employment and profit making adventure to both some national and international business men and women's interests for investment and reaping of profits.

This is why given this individual experience as another microscorm for analysis of many other youths' experiences, I can completely agree with the position of Mr. Linus Okorie, (founder of "GOTINI" Guardian of the Nation Institute) a 'promising youth leader for efficient Guidance for availability of leadership in Africa', that;

"the greatest problem of young people in our lands,

in Nigeria and even most of Africa is not poverty,

it is not unemployment. No it is lack of direction".

There can be no purposeful leadership in absence of direction and presence of endless politicization of national values cannot mean leadership, as I leave you here to 'ponder on' if we have leadership for the youth in Africa. Since one principle of great leaders is not to produce followers, but to produce other and more prominent leaders.

The radical statement of Vatican 11 document which states that; "where the youth stands, there is the future of Religion and the church" u . It needs no doubt about it. It is not right under any law, to treat anyone as a no body.

As one observes critically that some acting owners or heads of churches appear to be confused and the much they can offer their subjects (the youth) is an unmediated deceit. While there are other kinds of leading men in religion who may not be confused, but their actions towards the youth under them are un-God like! The youth are seldom encouraged by them. In truth, they do not respect or regard the rights to live, of the youth, simply because the youth have given themselves to divine worship. And this group does not care whether their actions are detrimental to the youth's future success or that of Christian claims and values. It is a set back to our world.

But this is very bad and worth avoiding as religion is not meant to become an instrument of frustration to people, but our people are making it such? They want to play the gods who are not to be blamed (some are god Fathers in religion, some in politics and others in culture). They have failed to be shepherds. By this, they are by themselves laying the unworthy foundation of making youth's clever devils like professional prostitutes etc. "Those who live in a glass houses, should not throw stones" - Anon.

When a religious leader frustrates the hopes of the young, without an incentive to begin life elsewhere, "Foundation now destroyed, what can the young ones do?" Is it to become evil or to commit suicide or to be violent to the society?

Leaders! Do not teach the youth to hate or become enemies of religion. Do not support any abuse of a use, for as a religious leader today you are called to be the gentle elder brother of all people especially the young, to do this well implies giving up any personal acts of selfish ends in view.

There is this greatest weakness and ignorance with which people are liquidating the essence of religion. By this, those who dilute religion's value for political ends cannot qualify for anything other than impostors. When they are now out of character, they are out of the usual nature. It is better not to be religious than to become an impostor in religion. For if by good life in Religion, the good people become saints and heroes of the faith, those who play politics at the expense of religious values, simply become Anti-heroes and objects of religious tragedy.

Now, in the Christian realm constructive critical evaluation of attendants to worship, succinctly reveal that; the number of women (who are easily tuned by emotional projections) tends to triple that of men. Most preachers take negative advantage of this to manipulate these human's emotion, as if religion has made natural reasoning in-active. Now, not all places of worship are appreciated as "the holy places, as a de-emphasis of virtues of holiness, pious life which define growth in spiritual maturity appear to be on the rise now".

It is to be noted, that a good advancement in balanced spirituality, will naturally checkmate uncontrolled pursuit of materialism in religion. But where is the balanced spirituality, which ought to reflect in our human characters? This is enough in itself to cure our world of inherent corruption, but when we disregard moral values and virtues of religion, how can humans be free from corruption?

On further evaluative enquiry, one discovers that the valid truth is not that men do not like to worship God or pay tribute to him, but that majority of them are still angry because of certain illicit actions of these leaders in religion in one time in life or the other, because of these devaluation of useful values, under the umbrella of religion. So many are filled with anger in the things of God and this is because of those who worship him as leaders, often the shepherds.

No need denying realities, for this is why those who understand the genuine truth see the need for the pontifical apologies offered by Pope John Paul II of blessed memory, to pacify those injured by religion over the years. Therefore, Christians and other religious sects both the leaders and the led should be careful.

It requires being watchful and prayerful to see that they are not agents of destruction to fellow human's faith in God. Let us remember always that religion is given for all humans. Human leaders are there to serve not to play

'the god who is not to be blamed'. Or should there be human Idols/ deities in the modern world's system of worship? If this great Pope apologized, who is that leader, an African, an Elder who owes the youth a lot…. But feels so big to apologize?, Let him/her wake up from somnambulism.'

Islamic religion of Moslems; may be given some positive points in the moral ethics in considering its modesty on how its women dress, while extremes need be avoided. AS for the Christians, the religious leaders need to care more if the women dress morally or not. This apparent neglect of modesty in dressing is not devout Christianity, for among men, it is possible that some will easily be seduced, and ensnared to sin by mere act of looking at exposed bodies in less-moral dressing of some less principled women. Godly Love is showing compassion to the faith of others, not the often noticed 'I do not care attitude'.

However, Christianity scores the other positive points in respecting the rights to live and let live of others. Elders in Islamic religion need to admit that they have not done well or done enough to help make the world a better place by not preserving the sacredness of human life of others. This is one clarion call for it to stop. As cultural humans, beyond natural animals, we need to recover from illusions of fighting for religion, slaughtering of human beings.

This too is a negative culture, elders in Islamic faith need not keep silence over this injustice to fellow humans, at least because God in heaven will judge each one, especially for keeping evil silence when misfortune is befalling his neighbour. Such is hollow-humanity, an echo of failed human consciousness to the dignity and essence of life. It is a betrayal of the unspoken covenant of brotherhood, written in the secret conscience of all the living.

Religion is too small compared to who God is, he who made the whole universe. In his world, water bodies are greater than the whole earth- land mass, where humans live. Water animals worship God, but they do not engage in religious crisis. For almost everything including prayers we use in religion are too inferior to be compared to God/Allah the Almighty. Our entire worship is mere anthropomorphism, meaning human words, languages and expressions of limit of his/her understanding of God. 'God simply is; "the I am", unknown to none.

According to St. Thomas Aquinas, "God is the wholly other", beyond all we can think, suggest, describe or even presume of him. For humans cannot know the God who never let them see and behold him, we only think and presume that we know God. Think about this, in the realm of science, true knowledge is impossible outside of the empirical (physical) experience and observation of the object presumed to be known, so also is knowledge about God.

One reason why Islamic/Christian religious crisis should end hence forth is seeing that there will be no separate heaven or hell for Moslems and Christians. Nor will God allow anyone to bring religious crisis or Boko Haram into heaven, and Devil surely will not allow any of these in the hell fire. Not destined for hell or heaven, so why is it allowed here in Nigeria?

The political leaders may be responsible, when some of them worship in the shrines of the Devil. There, they face a demand for bloodshed, this is cannibal animalism, may be why they allow these evils to go on over the years. They lack wisdom, when they do not fear God. The youth must depart from such evils, for every wicked person, end sadly and shamefully. Oh youth, follow your own life's inspiration, the Godly advice your own mind gives you, do not just wait for the elders, some have skeletons in their cardboards to protect.

Political leaders fail to sanitize religious corruption, when they are not Godly.

They take everything religious leaders say. In history of great leaders, those who feared God like kings David, Asa, Jehoshaphat and Josiah, operated a political theocracy meaning a government of kings who fear God as source of their Government, so they gave direction of best ways of worship without error.

They had an era of peace and sanity because they upheld religious reforms and purification. They were young leaders and they succeeded in avoiding corruption in leadership positions V.

In Nigeria, like in many other African countries the greatest fuel upholding corruption is because religion is also corrupt. They have been pushed into the murky waters, the stinking and entangling chameleon faeces that entangles like a snare. Proliferation itself is enough corruption, an aspect of religious capitalism, where almost each one wants to be seen at or as the head of a church.

Capitalism came from a Latin word 'caput' meaning "head". It is these struggles for head-ship that bring corruption to religion, making religious capitalism to take the place of spiritual life and devout moral life that should have ability to correct citizens and help them stop corruption.

Still on Character and Society;

We have relegated moral virtues and good life as things that do not matter, all because of search for money, that is undue love for materialism and materialism in religion is another name for religious capitalism. This is why the society is decaying; even the Philosophers are failing to point these out, many now lose their character, is it because the confused people ask 'what is your work as a philosopher?' Why did you leave every other thing/profession to become a philosopher?

Those who hate the truth, try to stop the philosophers from doing their work, such is why they fail to say what I am saying now, hence the society falls into decay, as it is decaying now and many claim each time that;

"No one can stop a society like Nigeria from being corrupt".

This is a confession of acute ignorance in the heart of people and it is in the duty of philosophers to cure the society of such debased thinking.

The solution to all of our society's all round problems, is not very far-fetched, let Philosophers be given a good chance and the wounded nation be healed, for the truth remains as Plato the Ancient Philosopher put it "there will be no peace in a state/ nation, unless philosophers become kings and kings become philosophers" that is the one secret to the problem of Nigeria, and some other African Countries. We are afraid of the truth, and often stop the weak from saying it.

But another truth is that science and development never thrives on lies, so also is this socio-cultural claim like the 'African time'. This badly affects Africans in social and economic development and we are falling apart in its illusion.

His Excellency, Governor Peter Obi of Anambra State in Nigeria is one example of a Philosopher in politics. Let us appreciate this truth at least we are proud he is a model for the youth, haven shown that boldness in pursuit of legal rights of individuals, without shedding of blood, can be carried out even when society is said to be corrupt, one person can stand up to show direction and many others will follow. This he did philosophically well.

This simply becomes a new culture especially in politics. That you can afford to be the first to step out of that insipid madness of corruption and remain successful in life.

People expect him to do more, and become a standing model for youths in many other ways too. In Social infrastructures like improving the interior/ rural road net works and bridges, he like Dr. Chris Ngige before him, left outstanding legacies. He restored hope in the dignity of education and health facilities and the land has peace in his day.

He like few others below, is a point of reference in

leadership for the future. He is a philosopher and a patron to philosophers.

Governor Sullivan Iheanacho Chime has shown great commitment in morally rebuilding of the youth he inherited in the coal city, especially his courage in putting to near end the evil of student's culture of cultism. Today, he is a youth's model that politics can stop existing evils in society and points an unspoken direction that every youth has got something to stop, put to an end the ancient existing evil in any situation he or she has inherited in life.

So do not pretend that it is a culture or presume that it was there before you came. What does not matter today will bring matters arising tomorrow! He has been bold enough in charting a new course to the wave of politics to ensure justice and fairness.

He is also initiating structural revolutions in the coal City State, by offering sound legacies in infrastructure provisions in e state, especially opening new road net works that were never there before and modernizing old ones.

Governor Rochas Okorocha of Imo state has demonstrated that pragmatism is possible in the leadership vacuum so far created in Africa. He, besides changing the status quo, has shown that returning to the past to finish that good works of developmental investment as in Agriculture and industrial development, previously started but unfinished by the heroes' past is the best way to consider integral governance in Africa. His attitude to education of the poor masses makes him a man-mountain.

Governor Babatunde Fashiola of Lagos State has shown another spirit of Pragmatism in transforming the once moribund and dilapidated city of Lagos to the present reminiscence of Lagos as the New York City of Africa. He shows that the good leader is truly the servant of his people. He is a humble genius.

Also Governor Adams Oshiomole of Edo state, has shown the new wave of genius by consolidating the basic rural development as a fundamental obligation of a quintessential leader, this is more honourable than the conventional penchant of limiting development like the road infrastructures to the capital city.

He believes in the dignity of the youth, and upholds that a people oriented government is the only way to remain relevant in history of salvaging Africa.

Governor Godswill Akpabio of Akwa Ibom state, is a one man too many in daring to create a new world order of decent development, far from the crowd of political intoxication of power, he bent down to the basic infrastructural needs of his people. He is like that leader in the biblical book of Maccabeus who loves his people and even prays for their welfare. His works speaks for itself.

Governor Aliyu Babangida of Niger has offered relative hope for peace in a field of war; he provided employment for about 2000 youths in his state. In him can be seen another man mountain who differs from the crowd, in him can be seen a will power to leadership, not lost at the banquet of political illusion when Africa is on fire of self annihilation. He also made girl child education free to encourage women education in northern Nigeria.

Governor Rotimi Amechi of Rivers, has taught and I believe him that; "We must create the African reality for the images against the 'black-man' to disappear". He too began with the spirit of a genius and offered his home state leadership pragmatism in areas of modern infrastructures in educational and health facilities. Good roads, bridges and world class educational facilities are good records that speaks of his works.

Governor Emmanuel Udeaghan of Delta State has left positive legacies that the young people are the best asset due for investment of any one in government helms of affairs. His commitment to micro-finance related support to the economic wellbeing of the young people of Delta state is profound.

Governor Sarike Dickson of Bayelsa State, has identified with an area of basic need in building and rehabilitating the image of the Nigerian police, restoring the treasury values of a human society by creating the new image of traditional rulers of the state, improving the road network of the rural communities and consolidating the lucid essence of the education of the young through awarding of scholarship in collaboration with NDDC.

Governor Gabriel Suswan has shown great devotion to peace and respect for the life of other citizen's especially those who seem alien to his home state is a hallmark of great leaders. His disposition in the areas of religion, gentle life, humility in political disposition and mutual relation with others is a model to most young people.

These few are some standing examples among averagely young leaders of states in Nigeria, perhaps who are presently known for something positive, (especially for not getting lost in the crowd of being politicians), that can give hope for the young. They show good examples that with courage and self determination, any young person can change the status quo, far and better than old traditions that exist in today's world for a new world order of goodness.

Besides the men, young women cannot presume weakness or poverty in anyone's background like the family as a reason to abandon educational pursuit or career development prospects for their future and submit to prostitution, as young women litter the city street every evening, imposing way ward-ness on the human society as a way of life. Yet, those who have fallen, can still stand up today seeing that they have got models like Professor (Mrs.) Dora Akunyili, who did not ignore the African moral values in her days as the

Director General of NAFDAC, she prevailed that fake drugs and evil in society can be abolished.

Dr. Mrs. Ngozi Okonjo Iweala and Dr. Mrs. Oby Ezekwesili are women who lead and highly represent Africa in leadership of world affairs like the World Bank. They had laboured with their youth to prove great points to men and the entire human society in their various capacities in political and leadership positions.

These are well perceived on behalves of all well meaning women of African societies that one must not throw moral virtues to the winds to be carried away into oblivion or to the mud to be buried as unimportant in modern civilization.

In these three women, every young woman or girl can appreciate that money, fashion and similar vanities that most feminine's pursue today in the spirit of do or die now, should not become priorities in one's youth. Everyone can see today that moral uprightness in women, even in men, brings one to limelight and even political greatness. Even under the influence of power and politics. They stood firm in their daily dressing like decent women of African descent, they show great direction in era of moral crisis, imagine their head ties.

Maybe that is the only character of theirs other women have chosen to emulate.

Today, some youths are copying the immoral life of Gay marriage, sodomy, Abortion, ruining the beauty of life

before natural marriage, to promiscuous life and
Lesbianism; some adopt artificial parts of human body,
like nails. Others tattoo their skins copying even moral
mistakes from the western world, this is not yet able to
and will surely never lead anyone, man or woman to
greatness. Some move around with unpleasant smell in
the name of fashion. But do they know that they smell
badly? It is a deadly stroke on life, because even if they
are told, they will not admit it.

African people must now work harder to preserve their
moral dignity, nothing works in life like self
preservation, and this is the greatest instinct in human
life. No youth will be right to presume that the world is
so corrupt, and can no longer be redeemed. You can join
the courageous few, as exemplified above to help as we
plan to change the world for good, everything good is
still possible, and African youths can live good life even
today, but you must play your own part, do not just sit
down and criticize others.

The Youth should not listen to words that run down
their inspired intelligence, this is one way God speaks
and directs everyone on earth, but some are afraid of
inspiration, hence they avoid atmosphere of quiet life
while others are ignorant of this, they keep searching for
religious and spiritual direction in wrong places that
offer youth's occultism and deceit. If you fear God, then
learn to listen to your own mind and conscience, you
will be great and virtuous for a good life is always
possible.

TEN | Education and Awareness

The prominent term education has its etymological origin from the Latin word; Educere meaning to 'lead out', that is out of ignorance. To educate or to teach remains a useful method of transporting and imparting wisdom and knowledge from one man to another. Owning to the infinite tense of its etymology, it stands to suggest the basic nature of education. It is therefore a progressive avenue of imparting knowledge. To educate means to eschew from annals of multiple ignorance.

There is much, which any age should regret if they have neither regard nor support for positive values of Education, for why is African problems almost persistent? It is simply because our people are not generally educated. Here people have come up with the impolite-empty theory; "Nigerians do not read books", This is a fire on the mountain of nation building and many are comfortable, that we accept this as a new national culture. As if that is our mantra for Nationalism. But who will heal Nigerians of this sickness? Our burden of ignorance, our logic of self delusion! The youth, you and I can do so even now.

Considering Awareness; one thinks of knowledge through consciousness. How are our people ready to educate the citizens in other to make solvable all these persisting problems? Why do we have the culture of paying greater attention to those things that are less helpful?

There are many forms of education, but focusing here on formal education which is fundamentally one of the important needs of the African youth, one discovers that following the sequence of civilization history in the world that apart from British imposition of formal education and that of some missionaries apostolate that gave it much credence, not many of our people here in Nigeria placed importance to the valid, relevance of education. Considering its missionary origin, we felt these values in the past, but have lost the trend in the present. What fate shall our future bestow? But our leaders have got a handful of the early missionary's serious attention. Now are they giving back what they received? Yet, if by any means contrary, present day efforts are insufficient.

Let us consider the intermittent break ups of the system because of absurd and inimical strike actions. They treat the education of our youth as a factor of 5th class importance. A phenomenon they easily neglect, forgetting that its consequence will boomerang on all people. In Africa, people who are not educated are silently in sorrow while the few educated ones are happy. Yet all men were created to live happily and die happily. But can an uneducated person attain this unique splendour meant for all? Or to speak less of the problem and talk more of the lasting solutions, if offered by an African youth can this piece of advice be honoured without suspicion? For in the noble words of Munford Jones: "Ours is an age, which is proud of machines that think, but suspicious of men that try to think".

Who is doing greater harm to our education? Is it the African leaders who almost have all their own children studying in foreign countries thus are destroying future of Africa by depositing the fortunes meant for the general citizens of our blessed continent to other parts of the world? In the way we are governed, they act as if education is optional, by making it impossible for the poor. They thus hinder the joys and powers of the paupers. It seems education/ knowledge is a property of the rich!

Our only problem is ignorance "That unhealed weakness in man" As two types of silent rebellions take place, here; the educated and the uneducated are radically-silently opposed, unknown enemies. There are currents of jealousy that flow, and disturb the peace, which ought to develop unrestricted joy and harmony needed for building up Africa.

It is quite evident that power tussles in leadership opportunities is a confirmation of this as some literate people may like to be worshipped by regarding others as less reasonable. While some arrogant non-literate pro-professionals often tend to overpower reason with ignorant ideas, which cannot contribute to any societal progress, when we appreciate that ideas rule the world.

The high cost of education calls for a very serious debt of subsidy as the highest challenge of any government in the less developed countries. This is why the famous American president, Bill Clinton in the events of his political manifesto, said; "What we need is not the government that will promise to do everything for us, but the government that will empower us to do everything for ourselves". Thus, pragmatism especially from education should be about actions fulfilled and not about empty promises made. It is a weak part of politics in our hand.

Can we all then not imagine why the renowned British Philosopher Francis Bacon also said; "Train a child to the university graduation level and you have made him a success in his life". He did not waste time saying that; "Knowledge is power, and investment in knowledge, pays the highest dividends."

What else? Is it a wise practice to destroy the rich values of our people's education? When the African leaders spend the public money in sending their own biological children to exorbitant schools abroad hoping that they will return to become masters over others, which is part of gullibility of hollow Capitalism.

Even if it seems good by its aim, it is wrong by its methodology, for we are all equal humans. The money may have been stolen, as in embezzlement and this is the basic and ulterior secret why education is drastically falling in our lands.

Education and Awareness

Come to think of it, these men we look upon to better our conditions are no longer interested, simply because their own children are not involved. Hence, anything can go on. These wrongs should stop for it is another unpardonable crime under heaven: "As few people have eaten the sour grape and set the teeth of the majority on edge". They forget that nemesis always follow, for how many children of wicked politicians are not wayward after all, they squandered public money on their families at the expense of the poor ones, life rewards them by making many of their children live in manners their parents are ashamed of, if truth be told many are useless, inspite of all those stolen funds, so, my question is; why is the wealth of Africa stolen just to be used in training children of politicians of whom many of them will become wayward or useless in the end? This same culture of waste will also be responsible for making other youth less useful, and unable to build up their continent and society.

Do not call anybody less privileged but critically oppose those who steal away their neighbour's privileges and devalue the innocent and moral persons. Therefore, it is time too to stop calling or regarding the uneducated youth as the less privileged. Our action is to become enough opposition to the wickedness by which their privileges are stolen away. For in accordance with the enthusiastic remark of late Bishop Okoye of Enugu, Catholic Diocese, Nigeria, "All that is required for the triumph of evil in a society is for the wise people to remain silent".

To be educated must then be basic and a way of empowering the moral strength of man. It enhances rational efficiency of the human brain to enable man remain the intellectual co-creator with God. Man can solve all the problems his world consist of, provided he starts and ends his activities with God.

Every man is a compendium of tangible and pragmatic intelligence and "knowledge is all about recollection of things already known to the subconscious" said Socrates. Socrates is completely correct as he massively demonstrated his philosophy in the exercise of knowledge (and) midwifery. For all people posses the required knowledge when given all the required assistance, they can deliver it to help resolve difficult situations. He opposed pedagogical principles and proved Anagogical approach to be better, by which education is a participatory process for all, where both teachers and learners share knowledge not as the imposition process seen in the old style in learning as in the pedagogy.

He also suggested that at birth people reincarnate from former world, so they retain traces of their past knowledge, now education plays the role of reminiscence/ recollection of what was previously known.

Education and Awareness

It is equally very wrong for the human society to determine who is knowledgeable or intelligent only by some insincere judgment of teachers and lecturers. Empirical evidence in life proves that not all judges are truthful.

A Nigeria prominent philosopher Joseph Omoregbe sums it all in saying that; "Any country that neglects the education of its citizens refuses to develop. For ignorance is a formidable obstacle to development". This is very true of Africa. But the idea of who is to be blamed or exonerated is a factor for each individual to contemplate, what is more important is who is to solve these prevailing problems? You and I can solve problems of our age, that's why we are here.

The youth in Africa must therefore wake up from existential and cultural slumbers. For it seems we have been practicing somnambulism, meaning a life of sleeping-walking. Our duty is to challenge our leaders and holding them accountable of the debts they owe to the nations. For it has been massively devalued. How can they think they are developing their fatherland by devaluing the education of its people? Yet importing technology that came from educated people whose knowledge are treasured in their own continents.

Why should some parents pretend to be teachers without helping their own children to go to school? The actions of some have made us to be regarded as unintelligent. Who made many become school dropouts because they have no money? When will this silent slavery stop in our lands? How long will they keep on enslaving others only to salvage their own children? But who among these people is not an African child? If Nigeria is the giant of Africa, its youth need to strive more than any other to ensure that their land departs from these limitations it is known with, and be positioned to truly stand as a giant.

This giant-ness must include being giant in possession of knowledge, to possess knowledge, a life of improved reading culture is very important and any citizen who ignores knowledge, or reading as part of personal development and a daily duty towards integral national development, has contributed to why his home land will not recover from its weakness and setback.

Every prosperous nation prosper partly because of great knowledge and skills developed by its citizens, its scientists and inventors, in Africa, lack of reading culture hinders the development of healthy national culture like discoveries and scientific inventions.

It is time for everyone, through an improved and government supported massive reading culture to help the giant recover from somnambulism.

ELEVEN | Politics, Control and Philosophy

The word 'politics; is as old as the earliest days of human civilization and the need for self-governance. It is believed to have been practiced first in the ancient Greek cities. It hence became part of early Greek philosophy. It is a social science that orders the principles of governing a state. The concept 'politics' directs the policies by which a team of persons orders participation in the affairs of governance.

The idea of control;

This points at the exercise of governance of a system. It refers to the act of regulating a body or group. Consequently, it revolves around the issue of right to administer or supervise social, religious or political power and authority.

Politicians are people who engage in the game of politics and their actions have never been the same under the influence of varying times and places in human history. Humanity has witnessed many types, the good, the bad types and their effects in our world. But our youthful challenge today is to rationally and critically analyze the political set up and development of the present day Africans, in this electronic age of ours.

The zenith of this necessity is to help politicians, to upgrade their way of thinking and moderate their emotional approach to political matters in other to rehabilitate our fatherland. To ensure that, "the labour of heroes past shall never be in vain". For a politician is a debtor, who has no other mission better than the business of serving and providing the basic needs of the governed.

God who made the world has the ideal power of politics in his hands. He created the idea of politics in man and Plato the philosopher modernized it for our use. But mortal minds know not this, here we see only temporal political mortals who neither fear God nor know much of what Plato modified politics to be. Therefore;"Listen to me important and public men ,

Presidents of assemblies give ears".

That there is no more politics in our politics, if what we have today in many African countries is our politics, for the gap between knowing and not knowing differs but little. Though all men are political by nature, not one is free to destroy the image and essence of politics in our world. For where one's freedom ends, there another's begins. And "the best freedom is that under law".

Today there is evil in our world simply because politics has fallen into wrong hands or that evil minded people have become advisers. Our world is getting sourer and youth's existence is constantly horrified. But these evils will not continue to prevail, if god-fearing people will be active in politics. The food for thought here is whether any man who cannot qualify as a 'god-conscious' leader should deserve the dignity that leadership accords as to lead a God–conscious society or group of people in Africa!

If Socrates is alive, he will condemn our politicians the way he condemned their Greek counterparts, if Plato is alive he is certain to prove wrong 95 percent of our daily political attributes, presumed today as skills. And if Aristotle is alive today, he will use Cain on almost all politicians in Africa, especially those politicians who have initiated themselves into evil and secret societies as their only hope of retaining power of leadership, instead of providing service to make Africa better.

Who then is free to destroy these classical and good political ideas they have consolidated, by doing what is evil in the name of politics?

"Oh present day politicians, what good have you achieved? Or are you alive to turn into bad the good historic efforts of the previous intelligent men of the ages past?

Many African heroes of the past did well to carry on these good political ideas. Now that they are dead, why did the goodness of politics seem to die with them? For every other good they could not do were politically done badly. As philosophers in Africa, we are all bound to correct the men and women who are misrepresenting the essential lives of their brethren.

C. H. Zudes

Philosophers are not people who beg to exist but are born to think out and re-fashion ideas just to help make the world a better place. All men claim to be wise, but only the wise people struggle to leave a better legacy in life than the situations they met. African youth are challenged here, therefore to become wise and not to go on imitating these evil examples of the older people, no matter who is involved.

As politicians go on with wrong politics shall philosophers not be free to do their work? And when this is done, why should any human life seem unsafe and insecure? If this is our political culture, when and how will Africa ever develop?

In Africa, her leading men today make no just use of either philosophy or philosophers. Oh youth, who then is ready to develop our Africa? This founder of the world's modern politics Plato was indeed right when he warned; "There will be no peace in the state (Country, Nation and even our continent) unless kings (politicians) become philosophers or philosophers are empowered as kings".

His noble dictum contains all the problems that torment Africa, as well as all the solutions that are to emancipate humanity from a wretched life of journeying to ignoble destinations. And emancipation is the clear goal towards this optimistic end. All the youths in Africa needs to learn to become philosophers' not mere orators or sophists.   No, become down to earth practical philosophers, the pragmatists. This is one positive effort, before thinking of leadership positions in politics.

This is one unique virtue I highly discovered in the former Majority Leader of Nigerian's House of Representative (1999-2003). Rt. Hon. Wakil Mohammed, an accomplished legal luminary and good enough, God has further elevated him as he is appointed by the incumbent Nigerian President Dr. Goodluck Jonathan, as the Minister of State, Ministry of Power in the year 2014.

The first time I encountered him in the year 2012, once he discovered I am a promising Philosopher, he naturally bared his mind that: "Philosophy is one field of study he loves and he is doing a lot to study and update his mind with its treasuries".

In all contacts with people, he is the first man that I discovered has great love for wisdom, unconcealed. A Great mind very different from the rest of men in Africa.

I then observed that: "besides the great heights he has attained in legal profession and political privileges, he was humane enough to reveal to me, that to become one of the best leaders of any society, he needs something that may be only a further study in philosophy can endow him and all men with".

I have silently pondered of him as one of the few most illustrious citizens of my country, which makes him one of the best assets for positive leadership in our generation. Hoping and wishing him that life will honour him more with greater privileges to serve humanity with beautiful benefits that are concealed in philosophy of his desired pursuit.

You can agree with me that anyone who thinks like him, if one day, is elected a state Governor or even a President of a human society/ nation, he will leave greater legacy of social justice which alone brings the greatest peace that ends wars even in the case of the present problems of Boko Haram and terrorism in our Africa, which appear to be more fierce in his home State Borno in far northern Nigeria for even to the fiercest warring States or parts of the world, any lover of philosophy is the best equipped individual to bring lasting peace, as Governor Peter Obi (the Philosopher) has done in Anambra State.

Anambra was the most politically volatile, boiling and war charged state in the years around 2001 and 2003 leading to even mobs threats to unseat a sitting state Governors in its dangerous era of god-fatherism.

But when a philosopher like Peter Obi took over the state, as a Governor, he knew what to do and did it philosophically. He offered the medicinal ointment that only philosophy contained to heal the sick society and eight years after in 2014, he left his world acclaimed land mark, which we shall not allow history to sweep under the carpets, lest we return to the dark ages of incivility. Today Anambra is one of the morally stable and socially harmonious and indeed one of the best states in Nigeria. I propose that this be done in Borno and other northern states in Nigeria, then Nigeria will return to a perfect peaceful Nation-state. But only when philosophers of lovers of philosophy take over political authorities of Governorship of home states.

I invite Nigerian Philosophers to acknowledge and honour Rt. Hon. Wakil Mohammed as a fellow of Nigerian Philosophers; we had appointed Mr. Peter Obi a Grand patron of Philosophers in our School days while I was the President of Association of Students Philosophers in the year 2002/2003 as its traceable evidence abound, even before he took on the Mandate of Governorship and shepherding of his home state like King David of Israel.

Many more than are countable have studied philosophy in and around African lands, but it is lamentable to discover that majority have developed and discovered nothing with which to help and alleviate our people's problematic naiveté. Why should the daily duties of many philosophers become the non-constructive and the less unreasonable critical devaluation of essential factors in the life of others? Why are you now an arm chair philosopher instead of a pragmatic philosopher? This makes you part of the problem. Do something better oh Philosophers and help build the age of pragmatism in our time.

Why must evil be part of our people's political culture?

That the few who make tangible attempts to do good receive easy gifts of discouragement and deprivation of basic forms of rights from the agents the government and often the self -imposed important dignitaries in the society. Africans have no place yet for securing the life of great minds that is why we find it harder to develop,

Our Heroes in Exile!

Since, it is usually the 'will of these heroes that constitute the wheel of history' in the entire human civilization. How then can Africa afford a healthy developmental civilization without indigenous heroes? But tell me who is it that is actually more important in this continent of our birth? All mortals are particularly constituents of both vanity and a periodic useful importance. And sincerity to our selves reminds us that no one is more important than the other. All men go naked to defecate or take their bath; at least this makes everyone equal in the ethics and principle of corporate humanity.

Time has come for the African youth who know why they are young and what it means to be young to repeat constantly to the political abusers of human rights; "I love and respect you all but fear not your guns, for my life began with a maker and to him alone, does its termination belong".

If we happen to imagine the adventures of those false-Africans who celebrate over the evil in our soil and who do nothing to alleviate the problems bothering humanity, many of whom have stolen from the wealth of their nations, if anyone has done this, though sycophants may share from the stolen wealth, but they always call such a man in his absence a thief. Some think that their evils are never known. There is no secret under heaven. For whatever any one has taken time to do, will in time come to be known either today or tomorrow.

In the name of leadership, many who ought to be patriotic have degenerated into stealing. Silent thieves in our soils! Some are selfish enough, who have stored sufficient wealth even for their unborn grand children while the already existing African children, are going hungry and starving to death of resources.

Is this how to become rich? Is that, the call which politicians are here to answer in our Africa? By stealing from your homelands, to preserve for a future full of uncertainty, they are men doing the works, which God kept for himself and left their own basic duties undone. For why should the living human beings be hungry and dying while people are here, preserving the life of those who are yet to be born (into this life) no one is sure they will ever come to birth. Is this not political foolishness?

"IGNORANCE FOUND IN THE ALTAR OF WISDOM".

It is not bad to work very hard in order to grow rich but it is a great evil to acquire riches at the expense of justice and by intimidation of the poor. Tell me, is there any man who can never become rich, and any man who may never become poor, if there comes to be a metaphysical change of fortune.

Consider then and see the rates of unjust deprivation in our society, for the hardest working people are not always the rich ones and the richest ones often are not the hardest working people. A comparison context indicates that American richest people may be farmers, and inventors like Bill Gate and internet gurus like Philip Emeagwali etc why then must African richest people be found mostly among politicians, if we are in the path of sincere development?

Self-praise;

Here is another vulnerable cankerworm, destroying the essence of politics in Africa that our leaders are engaging in so much self-praise, but are achieving so little in service and practice. Yet in African conditions today; our youth need leaders more conscious of the good things to do and who will allow the citizens to give praise when necessary. "People who propose peace are not men afraid of war" – Anon. We too can sing praises but only cowardly men will sing praises in times of sorrow. Ours' is still a sorrow to recover from.

But why must our radio houses become means of exaggerated and sycophantic praise to governors and politicians, even when they are offending the rights of the citizens, as many are abandoned to die in poverty and hunger in prisons and hospitals? If a medical doctor becomes a governor, should citizens suffer more sickness, greater despair and hopelessness under his tenure? They command disengagement of workers, and give their fellow men gifts of frustration.

Why must the retirement benefits of (elderly) citizens who have spent their youth to serve their countries be withheld unjustly and many good-minded elders are ending in stroke sickness? And as they die uncared for, their young children left as orphans, are never cared for by anyone. Yet, we blame our colonizers! Why blame outsiders? A greater part of African political culture today, poisons the minds of its good people.

Any political leader who falls into the hands of sycophants can hardly perform well as a leader. As the greatest among all the problems that destroy politics is the part played by sycophants. Indeed, no one who behaves like a sycophant is a patriotic citizen.

There is another group that hinders the basic development of the African youth in politics. Many of them are the ignorant god-fathers; others are called the titled men or traditional leaders. Some struggle to become elder statesmen, as often as they no longer appear younger. These seldom know the truth and if they do know it, they use it not. They keep on conferring unnecessary, perhaps undeserved titles to African leaders, who ought to be servants. By this they attribute to fellow humans, some unnecessary backgrounds that belong to God alone... These are ugly missions of sycophants and ought to be leaders who could have done well, but only to end up doing very badly.

Those who could have satisfied the basic needs of their people now concentrate on planning for second tenure. Is second tenure the solution to the African's need? A rational politician should play his own part well and give chance for others. All men have useful contributions to make if human history will develop. Let no one play the god just because he has the opportunity today.

Once is enough, for political genius is ability to do it well the first time.

Wise politicians will never do evil with their opportunities.

Let all men fear God, the world he created, ordered and controls prove that he is a primordial political genius. From him idea of power took its origin, (but some African politicians are serving the devil, in search of power or fame, this is ignorance, at least Almighty God promised in the book of Prophet Zephaniah chapter 3:20

"to give you and I fame to

become known all over the

world and to make us prosperous again".

Politics and Control

This is another place I like to quote the words of President Goodluck Jonathan is his youthful wisdom to discover and point out that; "his Country Nigeria have no strong or even (world class famous) politicians".

I make bold to add that this is because they seek fame and prosperity in the wrong places, may be in the hand of the dangerous devil, but God's promise above is ever sure to those who serve him all their life and help others to do so too. So African dear politician return from the deceits of the Devil and seek God alone. If he/she must be happy in addition to being successful fear God. God has done so much, he never praises himself, but politicians do self praise in Africa.

God has both power and authority, but he never abuses them, he is just and loving for all things and all people.

He is the model and an ideal for the political humanity to emulate. God is bigger than any character for politicians to play his role, even if everything about life is understood as a drama. It is an empty concept to play 'the god-father', in African politics, without possessing the true virtues of a pragmatic God in leadership.

For God is not a Proud God, but most people in elementary political powers are very proud, some kill their perceived opponents, this is moral weakness in politics. If God can spare the life and powers of the Devil, it all means he is the primogenitor of democracy and this has never stopped his supremacy as God,

so why kill what you cannot create in the vain and mere
illusion of politics? These are politics of shadow pursuit,
it is politics of ignorance, for what is it the youth can
learn from this, that is not evil?

If you truly want to be great, if you truly want to reign
among men for so long, please fear God, he alone holds
the secret and supremacy of power, some politicians
have taken refuge in occultism, others in charms and
today some worship in the church of the Devil. All these
are idol worship. Some kings before you did it, today
history hates them and scorns them, as no one bears
their names, imagine names of kings like Pharaohs' of
Egypt, Pilate the Roman Governor, King
Nebuchadnezzar, king Ahab and her Queen Jezebel.
God punished them so will he do to any Godless
politician of our time, he sent dogs which ate the body
of Queen Jezebel, what a ridicule to a famous Queen!

Yet she ended as a mere dog droppings of dungs for
even the earth could not harbor her in any tomb, or
provide safety for you the wicked politicians. No one
could say this is the tomb of Jezebel.

Only the few kings of old who feared and obeyed God
and found favour with him still have people of our time
bearing their names like; King David, king Solomon and
King Jehoshaphat.

So if you want to leave a name behind in human history,
avoid evil and do good with your political opportunities.

Politics and Control

I have a good experience of these as a student leader in almost all stages of my education, so even now as a retiring youth, I have good experience of what power of leadership is all about. So many ignorant advisers think that one cannot combine political leadership and Godliness, but this is acute political ignorance expressed by fools alone, for anyone who denies the Almightiness of God because of politics is giving account of personal foolishness.

Imagine the excellence and order in God's creation, everything happen in its time, the sun and the moon all things obey the order in creation, this is the true picture politicians owe to bring forth in the society, such that godless men and women have no business in governing the human society. If they do, then we have destroyed the business of politics, even before bearing the name politicians!

Is anyone still proud bearing the name a politician?

When politicians cannot yet solve pervading problems of ordinary human society? How can Godless men have wisdom, only fear of God begets wisdom.

Wisdom makes one to know things to be proud of and not to be proud of objects of shame and self delusion. We live in a world where change is always possible. The youth of Africa have one mission, to change the order of things in their home lands, at least stopping Godless people from assuming leadership.

C. H. Zudes

TWELVE | Economics and self reliance

To think of economics, one easily brings to mind a useful factor of social concept, which thinks of possibilities of solution to the societal problems, aiding the means to alleviate the cost of life's difficulty in existence, within the scope of production and utilization of basic needs of man in society.

Professor Robbins had defined Economics as: "a social science which studies human behaviour as a relationship between ends and scarce resource which have alternative end". While Webster's dictionary accepts economics as "the study of ways in which natural resources are used and how the wealth they provide are divided and applied as the underlying principle to needs and prosperity of the society".

Self reliance; is the human ability to rely on one's own powers of creativity and achievement without absolute dependence on others, like the government.

Self-reliance is a way of utilizing one's innate potentials (powers) for the betterment of one's society and one self. It is equally of importance in the avenues of achieving one's good name. A self-reliant personality will not believe that anything is difficult in life. He or she sees all possible problems as mere challenges, subject to positive influences of time and attention.

As this quality alone emboldens people to discover in themselves the best ability for all kinds of success, which some are often looking out to find in other people! Like in the case of Black Africans, politicians and any leader, waiting for the white people to come and solve socio-political and socio-economic problems of Africans. This wrong expectation is an act of human laziness, simply because we failed to be self reliant.

A society that sincerely encourages the self-reliance of its citizens will always find out that its citizens will always be the best powers in the entire world to rely on to solve any life's problem specific or peculiar to them. Imagine the place of China and India, they listen to their environment and their indigenous philosophers, hence they solve their own problems, now are paid by other nations to help solve international problems, like modern Economics, Modern manufacturing and Modern Medical methodologies based on respect for indigenous metaphysics of both China and India respectively, these generate wealth for their own economy. So, what are Africans doing with African potentials, is it just these empty emphasis in our politics of self destruction and pulling down our own people out of tribal and ideological myiopsm?

And if any African nation will properly and actively consolidate the idea of self-reliance, they will achieve extensive self-confidence in all their citizens, including those held in the prisons. By this, such human society will discover that man is by his extended nature a co-creator in his world. For every man in a society have the ability for creativity bestowed on him. It is by this self-reliance that men rely on their power of judgment. And they believe that what they Judge as true today can be accepted as the truth at all times in the human history, if it does not change. In spite of the absurdities involved, for "factors preventing human knowledge are many" says a Philosopher. Some of our people practice their self-reliance but not as completely necessary as the human needs for it are.

Combining the economic creativity and self-reliance in the education of its youth, any African country can possibly measure up with any of the world's prominent and powerful countries that tantalize Africa with easy fortunes today. For the lands of Africa are richly blessed to bear abundant fruits in favour of its entire citizenry in their journey for development.

One simple truth people do not pay attention to is that God is the greatest mathematician in history. And consequently, each time he created people, he has put in enough basic material for their sustenance in any society they found themselves. Why is Africa waiting for Europe and America, before they face the reality of self development?

People believe that there is treasure in clay, but why do they not practice what they believe in? There is need for Agriculture; which by its etymological origin from Latin words 'Agro-cultus' simply means the practice of field cultivation, a culture in the field. As this is an enormous practice in the entire world. Greater majority of the unassisted Africans are undertaking it but why is it that they cannot achieve much to project Africa forward economically? At least to feed all its hungry and dehumanized citizens.

Is it because African soils are not fertile? Are we not favoured to be free from constant earthquakes! Why is it that America can use only about four percent of its population in Agriculture, and yet they can satisfy their citizen's demand for food and even extend kindness to fishes in the sea? The difference is purely lack of pragmatism in African system. Constantly, there are wrong investments made by most government in Africa. Must Africans keep begging for what they also can afford? Must the black man keep celebrating the riches, which he has not acquired? Why must there still be greater thick forests and bushes in Africa but very fewer farmlands and scanty plantations exist? Why must we allow the extended virgin lands in African setting to keep growing shrubs and weeds not of much use to man, yet there is poverty, there is hunger and paucity of available ones make them very expensive, those who cannot feed well, will hardly ever think fine thoughts or develop the inspired ideas from God's wisdom revealed to them to invent or manufacture anything in the world of science and discoveries.

For if our people would learn to reason properly, they would discover the need to convert any land that can flourish as vegetation into cultivation fields. They will convert the strength (with which men do evil to eliminate their neighbours in the unwise culture of witchcraft, fighting tribal or religious wars and poisoning their brothers or discovering their political enemies) into seeing that at least, 90 percent of whatever grows on land is food for man. That will be the end of hunger and poverty.

The government does not just have to pronounce without implementation. They owe the citizens so much in their debt to completely mechanize Agriculture, which they seldom considered as an obligation before now.

The Governments in Africa are teaching its citizens and youth how to make elaborate promises, which are seldom fulfilled. Why are there too many promises that are never fulfilled? They tantalize us with hopes of subsidizing the agricultural production of food. How many hopes of subsidies in recent times have been implemented and in what country?

Why are we living more in shadow while realities are easier and better for us? In pretence they do as if we have no money to mechanize Agriculture. But who and by what means are Nigerian and African wealth taken away and stored to rest in Swiss bank and the rest of the developed world banks, while the much populace of African citizens and youths are abandoned in penury. When will African countries wake up to the truths of the situations around them?

How will they begin to discover that in our people's under-play of values of economics lay our problems, while in their sincerity of interest in self-reliance lay the tangible solution to all life's needs?

Why must Africans feel proud when they are hungry and many are too arrogant to go to the farm? The government is always ready to apportion the blames on the youth for deserting the rural villages for the still, poorly developed cities. But what indeed has the government consistently done to consolidate the interest of the youth in agriculture? Why should the youth keep working like machines? This makes the African man/woman in our generation look older than his/her age and fall victim of that unattractive travel to the grave, to join the ancestors before his time, littering talents and destinies meant for development to be left un-utilized in grave yards.

There is much, which the government should come down in practical terms to do so that the citizens must do better without waiting for the vain promises that are seldom accomplished. Yet it is not wise for any human to engage in agriculture without improving the fertility of the soil. As this alone brings results that discourage agriculture, so does neglect of the youth bring results that destroy nationalism?

The rest of the African nations have much to learn from

the Egyptian's agricultural standard. For though they have little or no rain annually, being close to desert region, but they could realize the values of the flooding of the banks of the River Nile. By bringing the water under control, they could convert nature into culture and were favoured with extensive and bountiful harvests. Consequently, Egypt became a land of the smiling plenty in agricultural harvest, only after they had the misfortune of flood disaster" W.

Today, in the year 2012, the Nigerian people has been visited with similar flooding like that of Egypt, everyone is busy in lamentation, no one propands any modern theory or proficient solutions based on ideas about how to convert these excessive flooded water into beautiful alternatives like that of irrigating the surrounding Sahara and many other deserts, for enriched food revolution in Agriculture. Not even any government has shown interest in building/construction of flooded water reservoirs in the deserts for expansive irrigation and consequent food production in the near future.

I herein make another bold step to offer my generation an idea I consider and call artificial rain mechanism. This is a modern concept I have been imagining its possibility and invention, based on necessity which essentially becomes the mother of all inventions. I know that in an age of pragmatism W1 as we are moving towards, it is possible to build mechanical water projectile equipments that will end up causing artificial rain in distant target zones like arid deserts. Given the influence of electromagnetic waves in cellular phones and other telecast modules, which communicate distant features as if they were nearer, one discovers that anything that can be thought of, conceived and imagined can be created.

I think today as a philosopher that Government in any and all African countries need now to seek for young people of any nationality who have shown confidence in invention and creative development of such methodic polar water projectors; which essence would be to compress, pressurize, and lift flooded water from point of higher concentration to several kilometers high, and redirect them to similar kilometers distant in the desired directions like Sahara and other desert regions of our world, thus causing artificial rains in those territories and evacuating flood and unwanted water deposits from endangered zones of any nation.

But even if no government invests to achieve this, I am fully convinced, both in the spirit of pragmatism in agriculture and determination for methodic inventions, that any day I have the opportunity to lead a nation or any human society, nothing short of this, would be the order of the day, there will certainly be artificial rains from rivers, oceans and seas, and other inventions like moving from solar radiation of today to solar conduction and solar preservation , and storage in magnetic devices to assuage the intensity of the sun, whenever the influence of the sun (or dusty wind) becomes adverse to the world.

Economics and Self-reliance

This is the kind of duty the Government in our lands needs to fulfill, to invest in, funding the talents and sponsoring the creativity of young people, thereby tasking them to come up with more inventive ways to help make this world a better place. This is a better way to redirect youths extensive energy away from crimes of immorality, revolutions like the recent Industrial conflict in South Africa, Boko Haram in the Northern, 'MASSOB' in the South Eastern and Militancy in the Niger Delta of Nigeria. The Arab youth uprising in Libya, Syria, Pakistan, Iran, Libya and Iraq conflicts against inadequate leadership expectations from government of their respective countries.

What is common is that leaders close their eyes, they allow older people who deposit the wealth of Africa in countries of America and Europe like in Switzerland, to keep doing so, and everyone claims there is no money to develop our home lands.

I remember today with nostalgia, how I built the first ever Leisure Sitting Garden, "Philosophy Garden" for leisure of students, in my University days as a young student's leader. Years later, it has become a habour of rest for almost every other department to make use of, without emulating such legacies. Indeed, no one bothers to know left this or any other legacy. We are never historic.

I visited Nnamdi Azikiwe University Awka in March 2014, on Monday the 24th one holding a brief meeting with younger philosophers/ leaders, sitting in the same leisure Sit- out I built in the year 2003, student of English Department came around and requested to use that venue for a prayer session. I happily got up and allowed them. I wanted them to be happy. I was happier that my works bore fruits and strongly bearing fruits.

However, I expected that every other department ought to have achieved theirs, after an Eleven years distance. The same day I promised the young Philosophers I can come back to support them do more when I succeed in this book project.

I can remember my childhood with nostalgia, how I carefully channeled every flowing, even bathroom water into irrigating my rice gardens, vegetables and sugar canes. Later on, years shortly before and shortly after my university education, how I became the only young man that goes to farm work in my home village. At least, I left behind Some Banana, Plantain, Mango and orange, plantations. There was the attempted Cocoa nut devoured by termites, and about 2000 pieces of pineapple plantations devoured by Earth-worms. Every seed of what I consumed is to be planted as a personal principle. I want now, to ensure that cocoa grows massively in Eastern Nigeria.

Some human beings live all their many years on earth without planting one seedling of orange, mango etc. Imagine yourself as a liability, on the economic set back and burden you bring to the nation's economy if you never produced anything for the comfort and well being of others in the world and society in which you live. From Africa, we can export every crop/ fruit and get richer.

The day I will lead any nation, society or so, every one of its citizens will surely have either a plantation, garden or at least some cash crop's farm that will readily provide periodic financial income, as a way of being self reliant and contributing to National economic advancement in terms of Gross National Product (GDP). This is how to make a porous nation most prosperous again.

An economic conscious country cannot be wasteful and they can always discover fortunes on their own side. While any self-reliant nation will successfully discover how nothing should be wasted. For an advanced rationalism will indicate to man how everything he can see on earth is meant for a basic necessity as a solution to a particular problem and nothing at all is totally useless. But Africans are yet to start implementing this kind of thoughtful actions; we are busy claiming culture, defending masquerades, religion and shedding blood of our ought to be helpers in our world.

No person, people or continent that plans carefully on how to build up their economy or become self-reliant will underrate anything or anybody at all. For what is not valid today may become the most valid thing tomorrow. Truly, no one is actually important until tomorrow comes.

Economy is the highest basis of development and self-reliance is the greatest key in producing successful people in the world.

The question to everyone is what are you doing to create employment and build the earth? But today, unfortunately the young people of Nigeria especially girls are busy asking the self employed personnel; "where are you working?"

Whoever is not working for the government

in their own thinking should be discouraged,

for that alone appears to offer easy money, and

more simply because the government salary comes every month.

Also Banks give easier loans only to those who are paid salary.

This is corrupt thinking, it is such that plays feeder to origin of oceans of corruption as some swim in today, there is no serious way of supporting investment in our countries. Who then and how then do we build the African economies if the leadership cannot make every citizen trustworthy and ensure they are credit worthy for bank facilities?

Such youth are filled with noise, seeking nothing but opportunity to make more noise, often celebrating the success that is not yet founded in their continent. What a shadow life, we encourage in Africa!

Hearing that what is hidden inside books is hidden from Black people, we accept it as a complement for the wise, how many people or government do enough to challenge and correct this? This is where development begins.

I invite every African youth to read the book; Cash Flow Quadrant by Robert Kiyosaki. It will certainly make you to think differently, and think like an industrialist who creates jobs. Young people must wake up and challenge the Government of any society they live in, to support the youth pragmatically to industrialize, revolutionalize and thus repositioning African system, mentality, outlook and economy.

This act of waiting for the government, or allowing the government to tantalize our youth with vain promises, of political propaganda is a mentality of people who lack the spirit of creative genius and who fail to know why they are on earth, this is why we live unfulfilled lives and Africa is worse for it today.

Those who constitute of genius prefer to create their own job, work or develop their talents. They use this to employ others, thereby helping to build the economic prosperity of the society. But you discover that agents of governments in the same porousity of politics without pragmatism discourage indigenous investors.

It is another psychological battle in this continent to discover that those who work as agents of government, put a whole lot of both energy and interest to contradict, destroy and even annihilate the positive contributions of those who are self employer, recently, elected politicians, ministers, civil servants in the ministries have enviously carried on with a double standard routine of keeping almost all the awarding of Federal, State and even Local Government Contracts to both ghost and other's improficient companies that belong only to themselves or their friends, where they must be share holders.

Here they both collect salaries and they earn the funds from the often un-executed contracts. This is criminal, a crime under the sun. A setback to principles of nationalism and absolute denial to oaths of patriotism. These have kept professionals who alone are best qualified to contribute to national development, out of job, so how can our nations develop?

If you point this out, they claim, "you are not in government". Is it this that Africans consider as being in government, or pretend to be in power? Is our Political Power for use to under develop Africa!

Imagine the dirty and brutish incident which took place in the airport road Lubge Abuja in Nigeria between the 29th and 30th of September, 2012. Citizens of Africa, in a land where many lack accommodation facilities, inspite of lamentation for African underdevelopment, closed their eyes, due to political wickedness and demolished about 350 almost completely built houses in a famous proposed Immanuel Estate.

A Project belonging to Engr. Emmanuel Mbaka an indigenous investor, who have in many ways shown great commitment to genius of African development, at least by creating employment for many African young people. The empty stories about this suggest that some politicians have selfish interest in taking over this piece of land; should it now be like the case of taking over Naboth's vineyard in the Holy Bible, facilitated by Queen Jezebel?

Let these politicians find out how Queen Jezebel ended inspite of all the glory of power. This is one way, by which Africa is backward in development today.

In a pragmatic society, those who are charged with the duty of 'Development Control' ought to move ahead of any kind of building site, to ensure that every piece of land is properly designated and well specified for the best infrastructure that will ensure a patriotic respect for the intended 'city master plan'.

It is also their duty to enforce it and insist that nothing is began without approval. This will save the time, resources of money and energy from being wasted, each time any form of demolition is carried out. That is what leadership means to lead society out of poverty and underdevelopment and not what goes on here. So any system that has failed in their obligatory duties should accept responsibility, not to fall on others as a way of covering nepotism and professional irresponsibility.

In the views of Very Rev. Fr. Octavius Moo, "African countries have capacity to be self reliant but for greed and lack of leadership-wrong people in politics- not necessarily the wise" our (black) stars are yet to shine.

The question to everyone is what are you doing to create employment and build the earth? But today, unfortunately the young people of Nigeria especially girls are busy asking; "where are you working?"

Whoever is not working for the government in their own thinking should be discouraged, for many, simply because the government salary comes every month. Banks give loans only to those who are paid salary. Who then and how then do we build the African Economy? Such youth are filled with noise, seeking nothing but opportunity to make more noise, often celebrating the success that is not yet founded in their continent. What a shadowy life! Hearing that what is hidden inside books is hidden from Black people, we accept it as a complement for the wise. How do many people or government do enough to challenge and correct this? This is where development begins.

I invite every African youth to read the book; Cash Flow Quadrant by Robert Kiyosaki. It will certainly make you to think differently, and think like an industrialist who creates jobs. Young people must wake up and challenge the Government of any society they live in, to support the youth pragmatically to industrialize, revolutionalize and repositioning African system, mentality, outlook and economy.

This act of waiting for the government, or allowing the government to tantalize our youth with vain promises, of political propaganda is a mentality of people who lack the spirit of creative genius and who fail to know why they are on earth. Those who constitute of genius prefer to create their own jobs, work or develop their talents. They use this to employ others, thereby helping to build the economic prosperity of the society. In the views of Very rev. Fr. Octavius Moo,

"African countries have the capacity to be self reliant but for greed and lack of leadership, the wrong people in politics- not necessarily the wise"

Our (black) stars are yet to shine.

C. H. Zudes

THIRTEEN | Development and Discipline

Drawing the general attention to development one will tend to look upon the situations and factors that leads to evolution of an organism. To develop a thing is to upgrade its standard by applying cultural ethics to our natural limitations, thereby enhancing its useful value. Development may tend to go beyond the ordinary and a thing developed may seldom remain what it was. As Christopher Columbus was the man who discovered America while George Washington saw to its earliest development. And so it is with Africa.

To conceive the idea of Discipline, one easily imagines a kind of training, which may be moral or physical. However, human discipline is any attempt geared towards self-control. Discipline leads to obedience and proper improvement of one's personality. Hence, people can only be regarded as disciplined when they value the training they receive. And this self-discipline is the greatest value; a human person requires in actualizing his innate potentials, as to attain the best of destinies. Oliver Goldsmith was right in saying:

"Organize your thought, control your emotions and you ordain your destiny".

Discipline in its etymology came from Latin word 'discipuli' pointing to ideas like 'student, disciple and learner from a master. You can imagine the disciples of Jesus. This is a factor of making people better, if they followed certain principles of life of learning.

Therefore, Development is a factor for making things better in life, which demands human creative consciousness to give all the solutions to the basic problems of life. While discipline is a quality, a character and a decisive factor that make life worth living for man. It then requires human acceptance to make life more meaningful for himself. In relation to the situations surrounding the present day African youth; there is no doubt that our continent is still underdeveloped and that at least, 45 percents of youth there-in are in one way or the other taking greater delight in more civilized continents of the world, for their easier access to more prosperous existence. There is no lie told if one accepts that one is easily tantalized by the fact that our fellow (foreign) citizens are cared for by their government. And that their society leaders especially as in politics and religion do not easily abandon them to frustration as is now more rampant in certain countries in Africa.

Evaluating the Nigerian situation, these things are true, but in the need for human consciousness for development, there are some youth who have not been working hard. We all should learn to work harder than ever, to see what to contribute in making the world a better place. It is a time to become creative with your potentials, not waiting for anyone to employ you.

Development and Discipline

Talent pays more than any employment in the world. Imagine Michael Jackson, did any one employ him? He from childhood he employed many people including his own father and paid them with financial proceeds from his talent. He too is a model to emulate, all the youth have a talents, discover yours, develop it and use it well and become wealthy.

It is little minds that forever seek for employment, even in their old age. This is a cardinal truth, imagine how Mich. Tyson the boxer, on Friday 30th March 2012, was offered an opportunity to choose between two cards, and win half a billion dollar. Yes, just because he had developed his talent before now, if his developed talent did not make him popular, no one would offer him such opportunity to get wealthy by merely making a choice.

In the views of Rev. Fr. Dr. Bona Christus Umeogu the Philosopher, priest and lecturer-friend of the author; "Never you ignore a professional's advice".

"Live your life in such a way that

you have something to contribute,

after all what matters is what you contributed".

He too had contributed so much in the life of others, he became one of the most generous lecturers to students, because of his self discipline leading to his actualizing metaphysical self development, by developing his innate metaphysics an areas of talent, today, his attention is sought for by people of all works of life. In his actions, we learnt that lecturers can support their students financially, morally, spiritually unlike those who corrupt the young students sexually or by demanding bribes, thus teaching the youths to do such evils when they grow up.

All the strength that can qualify a human person to become a successful person is already contained in every man and woman even more in the group that are still young. The age is gradually over for us to wait for the government to influence lives for us, as governments of our nations, do not seem to be very ready to help matters.

In Nigeria, we have a Royal Farmer and a successful agro-based businessman, His Royal Highness Igwe I.O.U Ayalogu of Enugu Ngwo (the Asaa, of Ngwo Asaa) and the chairman and founder of Phinomar Group of agro-based Industries and Farms... He is one of the most successful poultry and livestock producers of the Eastern Nigeria. From my child hood, I heard his name and he remains an enviable rich man even at a veritable grand age.

He made farming a hobby instead of smoking cigarette, weed, or wee wee and other dangerous-ruinous herb habits that many young people of his day preferred. He, in veritable elderly age, looks healthier and happier than all those who refrained from farming in their youth among his peers. It gave him leisure, wealth and many blessings.

He told us in the year 1998, how he laid his foundation as a young man many years before now. He emphasized that; "the youth should not be ashamed to find time to farm. That after he had completed his basic education, in those days of his youth, while his counterparts chose to work in the offices thereby waiting for the government employment. He chose to trade from one business to the other and finally settled down to farming". Now this has led him to greater heights than any of his counterparts.

I discovered that being creative like him, is a sure way of delivering one's family and generation from perpetual poverty. Truly, a committed farmer will have enough food, meat, even milk and honey, also raw materials for industrial development in abundance. It is the first principle of conquering poverty.

I propose therefore, to every youth of Africa; following this theory and pragmatism in Agriculture of His Royal Highness; Igwe I.O.U Ayalogu, to ensure that in your youth, you invest in Agriculture, directly or indirectly, since this is a sure way of providing a better pension and gratuity for your older age. It would then be better to cultivate durable long lasting economic trees, in an environment that no reason can make any one demolish of cut them down and in such number, and different species that in every one of the twelve months of each year, you will have three or at least two major products to harvest from your farm plantation. Such is the best asset to hand over to a future generation.

It is a quality way of stopping erosion of other natural crisis such as Earth quakes from coming to our environment. Indeed, Federal Ministry of Environment owes the nation a duty to champion this as a good way of encouraging decent eco-system and ensuring preservation of healthier environment.

It is not enough to do surface dressing in matters of environmental preservation simply because in the study of Philosophy of Natural Sciences, natural causes can only be controlled when you do enough of the right things you ought to do to avert them, not by paying politics' with national values or even exploiting the system by demanding money on defaulters or young hawkers on the street, when no one has provided them a better alternative to avoid hawking as prohibited.

It is a conventional truth that anyone who plays leadership roles without being a farmer is most liable to steal government funds, hence delve into corruption. Hence, achieving discipline and avoiding corruption like stealing, requires of every one to plant and cultivate, some plantations as a reliable alternative source of income. It is a better way of ensuring abundant food and resources for one's nation and people.

At least it is a common knowledge that many of the

youth fear to suffer, while some are ashamed of being ridiculed as farmers. The HRH as above admonished the young, who can, "to make out their life's fortunes in agriculture, and fear of God".

For by these; "God can always sow unimaginable blessings for any farmer who serves him sincerely in the lands him cultivates".

Imagine picking some diamond in your farm and growing in riches, only because you farmed. Earth is the richest part in the natural existence, even the wealth of oil as in many nations, are gotten from earth. Therefore, earth's resources are super abundant, never finishes. There is a natural underground fire that silently renews the resources of the earth. However, there are only very few people like him and very many others that detest to suffer unto success like him.

Let us then sum this chapter by falling back on a disciplinary approach to all these facts. The youth should learn to avoid all acts of selfishness. This helps no body. It simply does more harm than good. "Be generous in your life, even with your talent". You have to be selfless in giving to the needy. For by so doing many have helped angels of God, who rewarded them with many blessings.

On moral principles for the Young,

We now listen to Tobit an adviser to his young son Tobias. To him, he said,

C. H. Zudes

"Do not keep back until the next day the wages of those

Who work for you, Pay them at once.

If you serve God you will be rewarded.

Be careful, my child, in all you do; be well disciplined in all

your behaviour.

Do to no one what you will not like done to you.

Do not drink wine to the point of drunkenness.

Avoid excess in everything"

You will have great wealth

if you fear God,

if you shun every kind, of sin and

if you do what is pleasing to the lord your God" X.

(Indeed, with anyone who fears God, all things will end well!)

The most important discipline is to admit that no work, talent or personality is inferior to another. It is in this, the placing or pricing of certain talents over others, in an act of arrogant capitalism that destroys the world, where every undisciplined person is finding ways to boast that he/she is better than others. It is only this that starts every of these crisis in the world, leading to hatred

Development and Discipline

like in racism and religious bigotry. That is another business of ignorance; you can conquer it even in politics.

This life is not a competition, no it is a challenge. The challenge of life is to develop yourself and your world will respect you if you remain developed forever, the greatest thing that win you respect and generate wealth for you is to find answers to basic problems of life by finding the best of solutions. If you develop solutions, you are made wealthy for it and everyone honours you for it. But this culture has not yet taken roots in our continent, if not, where are the inventors? Stop competing or contending with any one, that is not your mission on earth. Do not emulate the politicians who fail to invest in the youth or in the industrializing of their own rural communities. They, out of ignorance are busy waiting for the white man to come back and play the developer, they play to them good-boys –in –old- age, presuming to defend a deficient nationalism.

They end up destroying humanity through nepotism they lay the eggs of tribalism.

Examine once more the present day's ugly incident of 29th and 30th September, 2012 in Abuja Nigeria, the blind politics setting back the development of our continent, how they demolished a great number of apparently finished houses in the Estate of Sir. Engr. Emmanuel Mbaka, 'the Emanuel estate'.

C. H. Zudes

When agents of the government who pretends to be working for the government of a nation that is luring national and international investors to come and help build the underdeveloped economy, goes on to blindly demolish, over 350 buildings developed by this private sector indigenous investor, playing black-man's politics against their own black brothers.

Some because of tribal politics destroy nationalized banks, Airlines, and Cement and other manufacturing outfits, these are businesses of other Africans. Is this what the black race consider as politics? By destroying its own economy! Who then will develop our Africa?

Why must you destroy what you cannot develop?

Who then will develop Africa? Imagine our black mentality!

Is it a second missionary journey of the white man that will develop Africa?

Yet senseless African people are comfortable banking the resources and wealth of Africa in Europe, America and Switzerland, while Africa remains bare.

This is a shame not going to be acceptable in our own generation of leading Africa.

Today, Alhaji Aliko Dangote, the group president, Dangote Industries limited has set the pace, for you and I, he dared in so many ways to live beyond these African limitations. He shows direction in our present economic confusion, one by showing the youth that they too can survive and compete among the richest investors not only in Africa but strives to become the best in the world.

He is not waiting for any government employment, he is not absolutely waiting for the government contracts, and he is not known to be busy shedding the blood of others as in the kidnapping or stealing from anyone. He is not waiting for the oil block to give him money.

He is not one carrying those burdens of presumed African misfortunes in his head, to hinder himself from moving forward. No, he goes the good extra-miles where no one has gone before to make money. This for me is the new wave of a new face of Africa in our generation.

The youth must not wait to see the blood stream of those who failed in history of leadership to flow on, before they perceive that revolution is going on in Africa.

I met Alhaji Dangote only once, I saw mobile humility and simplicity in greatness in him. He came up from an organized family business structure, yet there are many others who were privileged like him, but majority have carelessly squandered these illustrious African fortunes in shadow lives like taking over other people's women. No one will attain greatness if he goes on to destroy those values of African morality.

C. H. Zudes

Here is a man who is not seen to have much time for women, but he will be remembered for massively creating employment to better the fate of the young ones. This is the true meaning of leadership, for this economic confusion of massive poverty among the people simply said, means absence of leadership. It is interesting to see him point the direction on how Nigerians can stop depending on other continents for its oil refineries as achievable in few years.

For the younger generation of Africans to do what the past elders failed to do well in, is an excellent way of becoming models in our history often deficient of good models.

Alhaji Dangote is doing well and allowed to stand out today, because in his home country Nigeria, the presidency of His Excellency Dr. Goodluck Jonathan is neither brutal nor destructive to the economic survival of investments of his countrymen. Far from the era when in the name of politics, the elders allowed business institutions to go down, causing massive poverty, harvest of penury in unemployment and bringing a rebirth of economic disaster on African, just to hurt an opponent and satistify political interest of a few. Today, the African giant is in relative peace, when its economy and politics is being led by great minds of middle aged men.

This is the first principle of best required revolution in Africa.

Development and Discipline

This is one way of announcing to the youth and everyone that we are leaving behind an era of the failed generation, of men of gerontocracy.

Now to an era of telling the elders to retire, that the younger generation, in their vibrancy and tenacity can now better confront, conquer the unconquered miles and solve the problems of Africa, this in itself, will be the beginning of African pragmatism, which almost everyone dreams of without identifying what exactly their dreams are geared at.

This absence of identification of what the matter of the moment is, remains why the African problem seems un-healing.

Let us always bear in mind that the problem of African youth is 'identity' and absence of direction. But can elders give the right direction, if and when some of them are also victims of identity crisis?

This is one reason why this work still strongly opposes any old fashioned style of compounding the African problem by those who serve the government as in the demolition of properties of the massive poor Africans, in the investment of the private sector based economy, without any handy alternative or inability to classically be ahead of any corporate investor, through foresighted patriotic planning by any Federal, State or other Development Control Agents.

C. H. Zudes

The government owes a great duty, to ensure that no one's investment in our Africa is brought down for political reasons, and even any other reason for it, brings in economic sabotage, for many have been victims in the past and Africa is made poorer for this by agents of its government.

Comparable tributes to Dangote's must also be given to other heavy weight investors in our continent especially for reducing youthful unemployment, among them are:

His Excellency, Chief Dr. Orji Uzor Kalu, who for some unfairness hidden in this gerontocracy in African politics meted out against his youthful contributions to robust investments in Africa, Nigeria to be precise within 2003-2007.

He had to move some of his business investments like the SLOK Airline from Nigeria to some other African Countries. At least, he deserves this essential recognition for appreciating that African nations need development and its youths need employment, which he readily made available, rather than just taking his investment to other more developed continents because of these African injustices to Africans.

Chief Audu Ogbe had besides his political contributions, shown direction by investing richly in Agriculture, like poultry farming where his farms provide numerous employments for many other young people in middle belt Nigeria and its capital territory, thus helping to reduce tension of hunger and poverty in the land. Like him, HRH Igwe I.O.U Ayalogu has equally employed many young people through Agriculture. It is their kind of contribution I love to make too.

Chief Mike Adenuga, has over the years worked smartly as a silent industrialist in providing employment for teeming population of younger generation of fellow Africans, in both banking and telecommunication to mention but a few.

I invite you to observe that of anyone who developed himself/herself, honestly and devoutly for the welfare of others' and progress of the world, this life bows to him/her, even when he is in any political contest. He/She wins why? Just because Life is wise, and able always, to make your opponents inferior to where you are standing, if you have been doing the right thing you are destined to do, as in helping others.

African youth give pleasure to develop your inner potentials and Africa will be a most developed continent, given all it is endowed with, left in its virginal nature.

It is very important to point out this concealed truth of ages, that where ever things have worked and great development and inventions have taken place in history, it is Philosophers' who say what should be done. Other professionals may be the Engineers say how it should be done.

If Africans truly desires development, Philosophers' should be assigned their basic and obligatory duties. Only in this way can we achieve direction every other thing will end up as a harvest of confusion in the future of our continent. Even today's over dependence on invitation of foreign investors without a serious attention to basic technology transfer, with this attitude of demolishing African investors as examined briefly above, we need to make a turn around.

IDEAS ON TALENT! (My Experiences)

Oh youth, what are you told in your prayers? Do you listen when you pray?

A sage was approached by the youthful disciples, and they asked him what is prayer?

'Prayer is Awareness! Awareness!! and Awareness'!!!- said the master.

Oh Youth! What is your talent? Is it just this proliferation in religious beliefs?

Young people should seek and develop their talents beyond every other searching of values under the sun. You may need short timed prayers to help you discover your destiny and talents in life. Often it is important to listen to only those who sincerely, and out of great love speak to help you discover yourself. Avoid others who do not believe you are destined for greatness.

Development and Discipline

Those who search for jobs and employments should first seek the development of their innate potentials for each man is an industry undiscovered. When this self-industry is discovered, it becomes a vehicle moving anyone to achieve the success required in one's life. Your developed talent is the best thing to make you constantly shake hands with the great ones. It is the first step of great life leading to greatness.

Until anyone discovers and knows oneself, one may perpetually move in circles of changing from one job's non-satisfaction to another, where such a one may never get that job satisfaction, often, because it does not exist for you, when you are destined by God to create one with your talent.

Self discovery is the greatest instrument required to resolve the crisis besieging humanity. Learn then today, that those who know themselves have solved half of their problems in life. This was clearly brought out in the classic postulations of Socrates who said: "Man Know Thy Self". And President J. F. Kennedy who said; "Every problem can be solved by man".

From the ancient times, Socrates philosophized like the few men who saw tomorrow, and he knew before hand that if any one dares to discover and know oneself, it is certain that life's problem once discovered is half solved and as such the individual will discover him/herself as an industry with sufficient potentials to keep the world busy. Such a one would be creating business for others, and business begets money, therefore, talent brings wealth.

Money is herein presented as a by-product of economic creation. By this, any worthwhile thing/ venture that you can engage in which has both potential and capacity of solving other people's problem now or in the near future in society is surely going to bring you wealth if you persevere.

Imagine Michael Jackson, no one ever employed him, his self discovery in Music made him wealthy and he employed the whole world psychologically, to listen to his music and pay for it. This wisdom of self study is one ancient secret, of why some remain rich and others remain poor in life.

Now, best of what people really need is money for wealth creation, not just Jobs for employment sake. If you develop any God given talent, he, the owner of this talent responds to you in his own ways, sends you a helper, who will provide money in the part you move on towards your development. This is true to my own exposure based on periodic experiences.

So, let every young person, do enough of self discovery, self actualization and each man's problem will be half solved. Experience shows, it is achievable with sincerity and self examination.

To define and develop your destiny, through your talent simply observe your character from early childhood, pay good attention to those things you do with ease, passion, and at best love to do without stress and that which you may be best in of which no one beats you in it. So "Don't ever ignore your childhood", says Isaac Newton. Childhood memories are best ingredient to package your future with, to become successful.

A personal example is that as a promising author today, I had discovered early in life that none of my fellow students ever beat me in this subject 'literature', as in before a teacher could explain it, I have understood it and help the teacher explain to students by answering any question correctly, I did even better in grammar e.t.c

Another secret is that your character is your Destiny.

The character you build up daily determines your destiny.

Lastly, it is in my opinion that young people all over Africa do not just go on dancing the music of Michael Jackson and other renowned artists and achievers, they should also study those positive ways he grew up developing his talent even without enormous education, and he made fortunes and has left a good legacy for every young person to emulate. Do not just keep looking for this thing called employment; this act is similar to laziness, talent recognition helps people gain experiences and money.

'Pele, African football Legend' whose full name is "Edison Arantes De Nacimento" challenges every one especially the youth to; "Make your passion become your profession".

Understanding and implementing this alone is the fundamental secret of economic prosperity and greatness known only to a few great ones.

Talent and destiny:

Talent and destiny can be explained out in these terms:

Moses had the destiny and divine assignment to lead the people of Israel out of Egypt . He carried on with this mission. Observe then that in the entire history of miracles that was performed by God through Moses, that it was talents in his hand that featured for these miracles to come through.

Consider the episode of turning a walking stick into a serpent, God had asked Moses, "what do you have in your hand?" That stick was talent in his hand, a staff of authority as a great shepherd and leader. Talent is that thing in your hand; oh youth do you still leave yours unknown and underdeveloped.

Consider too the episode of crossing the red sea, that sea of reeds of ancient times. Ancient seas of uncertainty exist in many young people's life. Imagine that God told

Development and Discipline

Moses to strike the sea of reeds with that talent in his hand. When he believed Him, applied his talent to use, miracle of all miracles happened. This talent of Moses was used to divide the sea of life into two standing walls of water, sorted out by the strong East wind, 'Oh wind from the East'.

Imagine the above and understand that; God has already given you answers to your endless prayers through the talents he gave you. For if truly you (those who are spending time meant for work, doing endless prayers) have the gift of interior locution like Moses, you will hear God telling you the same thing by still asking you, "What do you have in your hands?"

He is directing you. "Use it" he says.

Talent is that invisible natural gift that complements and fulfils the human destiny, it helps anyone who utilizes it to break the red seas of life's problems, it makes confusions and uncertainties to give way. Xa It shows direction since your talent is an image of God's glory, unstoppable presence of Divine powers to make you create the world like God making people who follow you to walk on and pass through the uncertain waters of life, while matching on dry ground X1 inspite of the seas of problems and confusions that surround life. You can live without having problems.

Talent is based and understood from intuition as the 6th sense in you.

Talent is Leadership:

How is Talent Leadership? Given the persistence of African challenges, talent is that gift given to a leader, to help, lead-out, deliver from and solve problems of the people who follow them, to walk on dry grounds. When the people of African continent cannot solve these problems of life like poverty and other socio-economic developmental challenges, (inspite of nature's favours and fortunes), which implies walking through the red sea on dry ground appears impossible in our time. It is because the leaders are not using their talents in leading Africa. But can anyone use a talent as a leader if he never discovered or developed it?

If we lack good leadership in Africa, we simply lack a culture of developing and respecting talent and people who failed to discover or develop talents in them are masquerading to be leaders. This is why things are still falling apart now!

Today, modern African people need leadership contributions of men and women who offer service from the perspective of talents developed, they who know themselves, will certainly behave better than those who do not do order wise. Developing and applying this strategy makes a great difference between any younger crop of politicians and elderly ones who do not know that politics, leadership is all about service to help make the world better place.

Development and Discipline

An African author (in this poem) tells us that "Talent has a voice" but speaks not yet in Africa.

Talent has a voice

But speaks not in our land

Destinies like light denied illumination

Darkness prevailed

Oh land, your talents Silenced

Latent laid numerous stars

Of our darkest Nights

Ours had been battle

Against Humans,

Against Civilization

Destiny undeveloped, oh voiceless talents of men

Deny men ignorance not wisdom

Deny men slavery not freedom

C. H. Zudes

Africa, ignore your darkness not our talents

Talents latent in the world of prisoners

Talents, sleepless Sacred Stones, in grave yards

(Culled the Novel: Sacred Stones Lay Scattered) x11.

PART 2

What actually is love, where the youth are concerned?

Love is genuine, only when it is balanced

Unbalanced love has no foundation.

Careless love is like a house lacking foundation

If built on sand, no house is steady.

Do not be bought over to shed blood

No matter the money, power of blood will bring you shame.

Always remember, there is the powerful hand of God, for history did not forget to acknowledge, that though King Ahab and Queen Jezebel secretly murdered Naboth and took his vineyard. Nemesis did not spare them for the king had to die shamefully in the same field of Naboth and the dogs ate up the Queen because they once shed the blood of the innocent.

 Who then owned this vine yard now?

Be careful of whatever you say

The ears unseen still hears you.

Those who hide evil can seldom be happy

C. H. Zudes

By the love of freedom life's innocence is preserved.

Those who plan to do well,

Never end up in sorrow.

Success is a solution when it can be attained

When it cannot be attained, it remains a problem.

There is often more wickedness in homelands

And more love and friendship outside it.

In many lands and remote villages of Black people as in all the earth, people are more comfortable with remaining ignorant of why they came to birth; this makes them fight avoidable wars. They fight wars to possess often wretched inheritance from the dead. This has made many who stayed at home lands to die in vain. But many who left home to seek fortunes in exile have spared their lives. In one's youth, it is more honourable to travel away from home as Ben Sira exclaimed: "in my youth, before I went to traveling….."

****

Do not be contented with poor love in homeland

There are many unmade friends outside home.

Jubilee Harvest of Love for African Youths

Better love never won

Than such easily lost

If people have hated your goodness

Go into exile, before long they say; "had I known".

Do not give up because people suggest it

God's time may always be different.

The promising African young people can also learn this word 'my generation' from Professor Chinua Achebe of blessed memory, that their generation is different from that of 'failed generation' where good leadership remained a historic night mare of ages.

Knowledge of this difference can make ours different.

Do not mind the grand threats life presents

If it does not, how will you become great?

Cease to act when anger is dominant

No hero is known for his anger

Do not worry when people speak in anger

Angry mood never lasts.

At peace times people are different.

C. H. Zudes

If you think well you have no enemies

The angry brother can still be appeased

Do not be tired because of one ruined sanctuary

There is hope in the pregnant future.

Do not be tired of goodness and self-control

Even kings are admiring your wisdom

If you remain virtuous

Even your enemies will heap tears for their mistakes.

Never do evil to a just man

The evil you do can never be hidden.

.

Have you ever seen a broken bottle? Its content either evaporates or pours out in a mode of unbalanced distribution. Thus, have you ever witnessed a broken marriage in any family setting? Haven't we noticed old friends that no longer continued? Think of men of intellect who lost numerous fortunes in life because of love. Can we learn that with them love is not balanced? It may have been myopic. From such act of ignorance and much of human mistakes, love always repels. But if balanced, it will ever attract. For though we must love all people, love grows better when knowledge (intelligence) is behind it.

Human love is like magnetic wave it repels when, where and to whom it must, and attracts as such.

No negative - negative can attract or last long just as no positive-negative can repel nor end carelessly. There is knowledge that sustains love that is awareness. Just be aware that just as some must repel you, some must attract to you. When any love is not genuine better not be part of it. For in the absence of genuine love, there will not be presence of genuine happiness. Every wise love lasts long. It is not so emotional; it is not dominated by illusion. When men give credence to wisdom, wisdom will teach them how to survive more happily in this life. African youth should be wise and God-conscious in loving. That is how to develop their world and inflame their continent with genuine love and genuine happiness.

Parents at home should then teach their wards what love is and what it is not. They owe it as a serious duty to teach their children how to love God and hate no man, as our world is a home of friends. In the authoritative remarks of an elder, comrade Obunikem Asuzu, (then Executive Director Youth orientation foundation Awka Eastern Nigeria.) around the year 2000 AD.

"There is nothing bad about love or making Friends.

But it only becomes bad when the purpose in view is bad in itself. The problem is that often the parents do not know the right thing to teach their children, but often give wrong examples". "Young ones themselves must know that abuse of sex outside marriage is self-destructive. Because at birth God put into man a calculated measure of breathe to sustain him for 80 years and more. Of all the works that human beings do, sex or fornication takes greatest Number of breathe. The youth must then be careful not to shorten their life span, by avoiding fornication outside marriage; it will certainly affect their life span on earth".

If parents and elders should be sufficiently good, then we must change (the obsolete implications of famous human word "HOME" as it stands!)

H = for Hostility, O = for of, M = for Multiple and E for Enemies, to:

H: For Happiness, O for Obedience, M for Meekness and E for Endurance.

No place like home many people say, but is it so with all African youth? When it means as above, a place of Hostility, of multiple Enemies? This ancient claim can only become possible when our home becomes renewed as in this newest Acronym for a place of Happiness, Obedience, Meekness and Endurance for one another.

As many hate home for it is always on fire since it lacks love. Filled with wars, hatred and disunity of minds. Often this is hereditary, passed on from one set of ancestors to another and finally to their children, people are here to blame the youth, even when the only inheritance they had is relations at war of hatred.

When home lacks love ignorance is indeed at work.

Love is a parallel process. It goes on flowing and seldom ends if there is no sin either against the immortal or co-mortals. Infact, genuine love goes on as life goes on. Therefore, Africans should take time to achieve that love which lasts and which is a God-conscious way of loving. Truly, nothing destroys love as sin does. It is better to gain the new love of an old enemy than the new hatred of an old friend. Men should live both in equanimity and intelligence to see that no old friend will be newly treated as an enemy. It is wise to love those who love us yet wiser to help those who hated us to become our friends;

Our duty is to teach people that enmity is an obsolete language.

Or who has ever gained from his enemies? Has any person got any reward from an enemy, yet men do not engage in business without profit? Why then do they accept to play the game of enmity? No wise person is at home with this. Spend

your time in loving and you would have won the love of

numerous people to yourself, but spend your time in hatred and you would have won the hatred of numerous people to thy self. I have seen all this and it is quite true. Do you observe with me, that those who love others directly or indirectly bargain for love? And those who advance in hatred towards others develop into self-dislike and directly or indirectly campaign for much human hatred.

Life is a re-cyclic citadel and nothing is free in it, everything is interdependent.

Let us consider this prominent advice to parents from Javier Abad in his book FIDELITY...

"If love has died, then it is useless faking it

Love is not a matter of sentiments.

Now is the time to even be faithful,

and rebuild that love.

Love is not mere feeling, but the act of will.

To love is to respect the rights of children in the family!"

It is only in this that we can correctly give essential attention to the universal words of admonition of Joseph Omoregbe in his book, Ethics a systematic and historic study (page 172), quoting Seneca the Roman stoic philosopher.

Jubilee Harvest of Love for African Youths

"See that you are beloved by all while you live

and regretted by all when you die!!"

Indeed only genuine lovers and friends can be favoured thus. He equally advocated, "Man should master his passion and should not allow himself to become a slave of his passions or possessions. He preached forgiveness and benevolence to all men. And maintained that punishment should not be inflicted out of anger or from the spirit of vengeance but for the purpose of correction".

People who find it difficult to love God unconditionally, how can they love his creatures?

People, who fake love, dig their own grave. Faked love is like an endless fire the scorching flame spares neither the giver nor the receiver.

With genuine love, people build a nation

A patriotic mind is never selfish.

A selfish mind cannot love correctly

Such love is merely Myopic.

C. H. Zudes

If you perceive myopically

Do not speak of love

"Those who have not seen life

Become so Judgmental"--- Anon.

Those who Judge more, love less.

The path of love is correction and direction.

Each day Judgment starts

Love disappears.

Youth do not love because you desire

    Love just because you should.

Genuine love in youth starts from the family

Those who lack it never learnt from home.

Not all homes produce love

Hence, why it is not all people that practice love.

Once there is continued love

People will be gentle in counting mistakes

Jubilee Harvest of Love for African Youths

Love is correction and gentle reception.

Love is the basis of healthy family

As love unites parents who build families

Harmonizing love, it becomes one

One love is basis of unity.

Marital vow is that of oneness.

When families break, love is no longer one.

If a family lacks unity of purpose

Where is its love and what can it produce?

Many of the youth are afraid to love others

Because of the harsh opinion of elders around.

Such fear leads people to cowardice

It leads to immature actions in secret.

C. H. Zudes

To love carefully and wisely is not a sin

    As to sin is not an act or part of love.

 The happiest group of youth,

Are those who preserve love without sin

If you can love wisely, you obey God's Law

Avoiding love is not a true way to good life.

Better be the prudent lover who fears God.

    Constant reverence of God's presence

        Can preserve love without sin.

FIFTEEN | Love or Lust

Lust is an impure love

Destroys the values of genuine love.

Lust is a sensual snare, illicit

Pleasure that indoctrinates the mind of men

Ambition in heart's perception

Delusive in the soul's understanding.

All minds yearn for happiness

Vain desire can still not lead to it.

Pleasure is clothed in garment of thought

Our eyes are equally guilty for perceiving wrongs.

Vain desires of the flesh

Can hardly be answer to youth's need for happiness.

Happiness is an enduring virtue; it is dipper than fantasy of fading pleasures. It is a reward which follows naturally as a result of accomplishment of one's basic duty. No one can afford to be happy if he departs from the mission that corporate human destiny assigns him or her to carry out and help make the world a better place.

Essence of boy and girl relationship

Is poisoned by lust in mind

    Those who worship the flesh

        End up in vain actions of lust of the flesh.

When genuine love is invoke

    The youth go spiritual

    If lust is invoke, youth aim at carnal feelings.

Those who cherish discipline, can love genuinely

Those who hate it are easy victims of lust.

In sin, man loses the virtues of happiness.

When we lose happiness, what do we possess?

Some youth are contented with pleasure

Mere pleasure kills and never helps

Pleasures in man's life need control

Untamed pleasure plots our self-ruin.

Love or Lust

About self control,

Ben Sira admonishes thus;

"Do not be governed by your passions restrain your desire

If you allow yourself to satisfy your desire, this will make you the laughing stock of your enemies. Do not indulge in luxurious living. Do not get involved in such societies. Do not beggar yourself by banqueting. On credit when there is nothing in your pocket. A drunken workman will never grow rich. And one who makes light of small matters gradually sinks. Wine and women corrupt intelligent men. The customer of whores loses all sense of shame. And the man who knows no shame will lose his life.

Flesh and blood thinks of nothing but evil

And all of us are only dust and ashes" Y

> Common love among youth is of pleasure
>
> And careless pleasure multiplies sin
>
> Those who grow in pleasure
>
> Achieve love of utility
>
> This itself fades when utility is no more
>
> Do you call such love?

C. H. Zudes

Only a kind of love is necessary

It is the love of the good life.

Those who love the good are constant

They rise to useful virtues.

Love of the good is an intensive love

Once goodness abounds, love remains.

A good lover aims not in sin

This group is always happy

Therefore, do well and avoid evil, for only the good man can live a happy life.

Consider the classical story of Macbeth in the prophecy of the three witches, in the works of William Shakespeare. He was told he would be the next king. He would have been a happy king after proving triumphant in the war. But he lost the dignity of happiness, in his lust for political power. In this, he killed king Duncan. When he killed the elderly king in his sleep. The story became that Macbeth will sleep no more, because he had murdered sleep.

Now, selfishness through his wife had blinded his capacity for patience and respect through patriotism and love for the old king. If he had kept on, the path of love, and loyalty for the kingdom, he would have ended well. In this absence of genuine love, the name Macbeth became a tragedy, avoided by all people, no one answers it today. Lust destroyed the great man in him, if not; he would have been upheld as one of the greatest warrior-heroes in human history.

King David was a prominent one, but lust nearly ruined his greatness. Jesus reigns supreme everywhere today, simply because his love is not lustful. What a lesson for politicians of our time.

Through love people can achieve

The highest mission of life.

Living the good loving – life

Is achieving the True Life.

True life is a philosophic love

No practical Philosopher can ever be lustful.

Some love vanities.

And these sin, because of vain things.

The more our sins abounds

The more our love dies.

Un-moderated love is dangerous.

Its danger is equal to death.

C. H. Zudes

The higher point of love between Romeo and Juliet was fair, yet a dangerous experience. For this level of love without thinking, more lives were lost and both of them still found themselves in the grave in the cold hands of death. However, the positive powers in love had made the two kingdoms of their angry and gerontocratic parents to swear an oath of love. They could finally live in peace, but great Romeo and the greatest Juliet were no more. Their names lives on, every one answers it since they believed in love.

Those who love money love less of life.

"For in riches people lack wisdom".

Those who lust for riches,

Are rich in wealth but poor in generosity.

Being generous is a step to loving without lust

When there is no giving, there may be no loving.

But in giving without loving

Neither the giver nor receiver can be happy.

If our world is a home of love

Then the poor will exist like others.

Love or Lust

Imagine the politicians of the outgoing generation of our continent, how daringly, people lust for power. Some there-in forget why they were created, others in occultism, deny their creator while some in Machiavellian behaviour, kill the innocent like Macbeth. When they have murdered peace and happiness, how can they have peace? If they have no peace, how can the land of Africa and its youth know peace? It this lust for vanities is the problem of humans.

If you neglect the poor for their poverty.

Do you actually love the rich or their riches?

The lust for wealth by some humans

Is the foundation of poverty on others!

If you cannot give from your riches

Are you going to give from your poverty?

A poor man can still be a giver

A wise person always has a thing to offer.

When you cannot offer gifts

You may be a rich giver of greetings.

A humble man is generous with greetings.

A humble man's path is decorated in love.

C. H. Zudes

Love by humble people is a decorated Jewel

No man thus humble falls into the agony of sin.

Mother Theresa in Indian was never rich, she gave the
world her gift of service to humanity in humility and
Blessed Iwene Tansi was not rich and had no political
powers, yet he was the first to put Nigeria's name in the
list of nations with capacity to produce saints.

A state of sin is a delusive dungeon

Why fall into it in the name of Love?

A kind of Lovers abandons another in this depth

No sinful Lover remains in misfortune.

Do you know that sin is an illusion?

> What you perform in the morning,

> get tired of in the noon

Only to regret it in the evening.

Some youth delight to perform it in the Night.

Only to lose the awakening blessing of the new day.

Can my fellow youth love without sinning?

That is a way of preserving the values of love.

Love or Lust

A life of passion is existence in ignorance

Passionate lovers love nothing but illusion.

Imagine the male politician who invests the nation's wealth in modern women who in their youth or old age he has encouraged to play the role of prostitutes, or the young religionist' who move from one belief to another without readiness for stability in one's youth. What factor of greatness can they be remembered with, in their older age when the strength of youth is no more in them?

A sinful country is home of wrong lovers

If there is no sin, a person's action is correct.

Shall the countries not exist happily?

If there are no sex workers!

Why are some youth not aware?

Of their lives true missions?

For their beauty of life,

They sacrifice at the altar of Vanity.

For this money which satisfies no one

Why are some sacrificing their life's splendour?

C. H. Zudes

If there is no lust, will there not be life?

But if there is no love, life will lose meaning.

Love is not lustful

And lust can never become love.

A happy life is ever free from inordinate desires.

The world can still be a home of peace

If people can grow tired of sin

There is a handsome virtue that commands admiration.

A life of holiness and purity of heart.

Some are victims of vices!!

The carnal and impure thoughts of people.

Love gained as strength, may be lost in lust

Kindness sows the seed of love.

A happy life is ever free from inordinate desires

SIXTEEN | Friendship and Love

Friendship exists but not with all people,

Not at all times and not in all places.

It is a wonderful relationship among people.

It is a way of remaining good to all things

And never becoming bad to any,

Friendship is a benevolent extension

Of favours and kindness for the welfare of others

Friendship is likeness, when it grows it becomes love.

When it fades, it becomes hatred.

Friendship is a way of remaining generous

To the needs of the needy

It is a way of kindness, which knows no limits.

Good friends exist as a parallel process.

It provides awareness that

All friends are not the same.

C. H. Zudes

Friendship often starts in time of joy and

Not always continued in time of sorrow.

Even the famous Julius Caesar mistook political sycophancy as friendship.

This is how Brutus found it easy to betray and murder him.

Bad friends exist and they poison the aim of friendship

    The good friends renovate time of sorrow to joy.

Better the friends who teach what is good

Avoid those whose discussions lead to evil

A good friend exists not without trial.

The world is a home of friends, just because

No man's destiny is to become an enemy. But

If Julius Caesar in history examined his friends

He would be wise to beware of all, 'even you Brutus'.

Many admirers are bound to speak

But not all friends qualify for advisers.

Friendship and Love

Better a few advisers

    Yet a hand full of friends

No wise man hurries to trust friends,

Yet, no wise man refuses all, trust.

Hours of misfortune portray the qualities of our friends.

A day of trouble proves a friend in deed.

It is better to offend your friends

By saying the Truth

Than pretentious pleasures

Which men found on lies

Better the true friend whose words seem bitter

Than the fake friends whose words appear sweet.

A genuine friend is your second self.

They make up for what you lack.

Good friends love what you love, they care

For what you care and avoid what you avoid.

C. H. Zudes

Friendship remains incomplete outside generosity.

A generous friend enriches and never impoverishes.

Jesus of Nazareth died on the cross for all people, especially those who admit his friendship. He did for them on the road to Calvary what no one is known to have done for friends. He died that they may live; this love gave him vigor, amidst pomp and pageantry that surrounds his resurrection on the third day.

There is a better friend who opposes your likes

Such friends aim to make you better.

Never desert a poor friend, your friendship is

      With the personality not with his poverty

A kind of friend will command your servants.

      In their hearts some question

      Why you must be served.

Beware of whom you call a friend

Thus, you keep clear of your enemies.

In Godly friends' men find a treasure.

Fear God and you will be blessed

Friendship and Love

With many true friends.

Each time you rejoice among friends remember

Your end and you will avoid sin.

Many young people have a broken life because of the word 'love' and the concept' friendship'. They met the impostors who claim   what they are not. No genuine love will break another's life and all good friends heal the pains of life.

A holy friend is a house of defense.

Treasure of holiness is much beyond price.

Some men are so called but can hardly be friends

They are not friends, who hate your wisdom

This group will call you ignorant just to be happy

Some friends love what you have and

These hate who you are.

I have seen those who destroy their saviours

Indeed, so are some friends.

A wise friend will avoid gossip.

C. H. Zudes

No friend who gossips can be trust worthy

Choose friends among the moral ones

Select companions from the simple ones

My pen once brought a man great honour

His own pen brought me the greatest dishonour.

I saved those who deserved no saviour

They ruined those who deserved no ruin.

Another tragedy was reminiscence in 'Thing Fall Apart' because the hero was told but he did not listen to the fact that; "this Child calls you father, do not put hands in his death". The down fall of the hero, Okonkwo began once he put his hand in the death of one who called him father and took him for a friend!

So some Grey hairs tell lies to ruin a friend

They are destroyers and never friends.

Some wise friendship last forever

These wisely bring fortune to future generation.

A holy man cannot keep a sinful friend

A sinful friend is not friendly to the saintly.

Friendship and Love

Pessimism makes friendship subjective

Optimism proves friendship as universal.

They have more friends who think about others

    They make more enemies who think of themselves

  A humble friend cannot be selfish.

  A selfish friend is evenly arrogant.

  A dying friend pronounces blessings

  A dying enemy is an orator of curses.

The sick and prisoners are friends to all men

    The Rich and rulers befriend only a few, why?

    Better a sick one with friends

    Than a healthy Doctor with many enemies.

Friends of God are always happy

    Friends of the Devil know no joy.

Better a small friend caring like an elder

Than an elder misbehaving like children

This life is an illusion, there-in

Make no enemies for nothing

History is repeated with stories; one of them is of a great man with many powers, a great flock he shepherds. He had expelled a young man from a system that ordinarily offered the youth hope. He was not considered nor compensated. No one bothered about what happened to such young people.

No one knows that many years after, when the great one had taken to ill health, it was the young one who is now a medical doctor that was to operate on him.

The allusions of history, suggest that the young one who was then the Doctor, took revenge of the past abuse meted out on him and the grand old leader of the flock could not make it alive. This certainly would put the entire flock into confusion, because what they once felt it did not matter, it now brought matters arising. Everything yesterday and today has a flash back at tomorrow.

If you love God, your friends be many,

Many hate those who hate God.

Old friends beget a lasting flavour

Indeed, like the new wine they gladden the heart.

Friendship and Love

Keep no enemies on this road to life.

You never can tell through whom you part from life.

Sweetest friends illuminate as diamonds

   Often found among the God-fearing and upright ones.

Many friends may share your table

But not all that glitters is golden.

   In prosperity, none can tell his true friends

For sycophants abound, pretentious enemies abound

"Truly in riches, many men lack wisdom".

Is this not why many who have stolen the wealth of their nations, starving their fellow humans hardly now behave like human beings. So many of them behave no better than animals in the forest. Imagine king Nebuchadnezzar a lion in the forest for seven full years. Yet he was a political heavy weight, a king in his time.

   Some are easily deceived by bad friends.

   In days of adversity a bad friend is proved

In your misfortune in life, enemies speak boldly.

Many shout to hallow your name

C. H. Zudes

Yet, they plot to ruin your life.

Enmity is ignorance advanced

None who reasons properly partakes of it

This blindfolds all who are so weak in love.

If you create friendship,

Friends continuously come your way.

If you care for friends, they are bound to appreciate.

A few pray for your prosperity.

Multiply your friends

By this, you reduce your enemies.

I was taught in school never to get tired of making friends. I above all swore never to be a bad friend to anyone, rather let me never be a friend at all. Friendship is a dignified concept, not many things people do can qualify for it.

Be friendly to all men, then

You will have access to all knowledge

Respect your friends

All who love you will respect you in return.

Friendship and Love

A pretentious friend

Lacks love and needs to be taught wisdom

If you can care for the sick

Then you can maintain all friends.

If you can visit and do so to the prisoner

Then you can convert your enemies.

The best time to note your friends.

Is never in your prosperity

"Because in riches men lack wisdom."

Not all can think correctly.

Avoid promises to please a friend.

For by such, men create enemies.

King Harold lovingly admired the good works of John
the baptize, but to preserve his political position he
confined him in prison. In his personal determination,
he was concerned about releasing him, but the wife
hated John for his preaching embarrassed her

adulterous actions. The king's promise to a little dancing -girl made the king behead John, that same greatest preacher he admired and loved to set free.

If by truth you offend a friend, worry not

 From their conscience they will return to you.

Yet gentleness is an obligation

If friendship must be preserved

Enemies project malice

Friends correct with moderacy.

To an enemy, your blood counts for nothing

                              To the good friend your blood
remain precious

Do not fear enemies

Conquer them with goodness

When a man is good, enemies multiply

When he is bad enemies are few (why)?

Friendship and Love

If you are a leader watch your advisers

For great sycophants become enemies in future.

If you think well you will become friendly

If you do not think, thinkers seem as your enemies.

SEVENTEEN | Adventures of Love

If love is an adventure

It means love can be dangerous

    God uses it to develop man

The devil uses it to destroy men

Do you know, many have fallen

Because they thought they love.

It is then better to grow strongly spiritual,

    in order to love correctly.

Love itself is a spiritual phenomenon

Not all can value it.

Yet, all are commanded to practice it.

The Adventure of love is an

Opportunity for the wise

C. H. Zudes

This danger is a golden one. It deprives

Some and empowers others.

Young biblical Esther was wise; she saw and used as golden opportunity when the heart of the king went for her, though she was an orphan, wisdom made her to become a Queen. But Queen Vashti played with fire, by embarrassing her man, the king. Esther was wise here, but the Queen was a simpleton in face of love.

For this Adventure, a wise person will fear God. By so doing all events will lead to happiness

A wise person sees danger and hides

A simpleton goes on and is crushed by it.

What can help a people hinders some people.

Wisdom devalues danger

And all love bows at wisdom's command.

None reasonable refuses to love the wise

Better to lack wisdom than to waste it.

A man with wisdom does not go in search of love.

Wisdom will notice love and obey its command.

Adventures of Love

So was it that the Queen, inspite of her old age, had no wisdom which Esther in her youth possessed. The king was wise, he did not have to go in search of Vashti's love, he used his powers and Esther replaced the older Queen.

Solomon was a great king, made famous by his wisdom. Wisdom alone attracted the love, jewels, gold and friendship from the Queen of Sheba. Everyone loved Solomon that he never went to wars because of wisdom. Kings and Queens who ought to have made wars on him brought him gifts. Cedars and Silver was made common and neighbouring nations considered him a Supreme ruler of all kings. ZC

If you love wisely

You will have no problem.

Truth and respect

These empower the lasting value of love.

A group is forcing love on the other

This is how men bargain for an adventure

The unwise forces love, which is emotional

The wise is still but commands it

C. H. Zudes

If you are not in-love do not be sad

Your solution is to wear the garb of wisdom

If you are not hated do not rejoice

All you need to do is stand firm in wisdom and goodness

Love is dangerous

For it has killed some youths

Outside danger its goodness exists and gladdens the heart.

If you can love all people

Then you will be free from danger

The love of the unknown places compelled Christopher Columbus to discover the unknown island, the south Indies that became today's America, our World's centre of civilization. Truly, without his yesterday's love for the unknown, there would be no today's America. Columbus founded a new world without firing or killing anyone. This is the greatness of love. A model to our time.

Those who kill their friends

Can never know peace

Adventures of Love

If you endanger your friends

How can you be free from the path of danger?

The salvation of love is bright as daylight

The danger of love is as dark as darkest night

Boy and girl relationship

Is a common instance of loves dangerous path

Many youth live in illusion

And some make mistakes in the illusions of love

Some parents encourage these mistakes

If they refuse to teach the youth about relationship

A country without sincere sex education

Neglect a great value in human development.

Education is incomplete

When it lacks lesson in psychological values of life

For Education to be integral

C. H. Zudes

It needs to incorporate sex education of the young

When government and teachers neglect sex Education, they deepen the dangers of love for the youth. (Sex) Education should incorporate divine intention, it is incomplete that which neglects God's commandment.

The psalmist asked; how can the young remain sinless? He offered the answer; by keeping God's commandments.

Youth who know better

Should wisely enlighten their colleagues.

For knowledge shared is knowledge multiplied

For knowledge is innate in all men.

What is sexual chemistry? A youth asked

Her colleagues refused to answer for they know it not.

It is not good for ignorance to be common

For suitable knowledge of basic factors

These save life from danger

Better the youth saved by knowledge

Adventures of Love

Yet, some young people are ruined by knowledge

When they tell dirty tales about sex

It is better and wiser to teach

"How to be pure, chaste and holy"

Than for government to teach the use of condom

EIGHTEEN | Wounds of Love

There would have been peace

If there were no hatred

Those who have no option than to hate

Have no option than to be peace-less

A peaceful home has no space for hatred.

Those who renew love with hatred miss the path of Life

Where there is no love and no Joy.

Indeed, there is no progress.

Imagine if your country is Nigeria, where the national spirit is fractured in the selfish thinking of tribalism, and most civil employed citizens are guilty of nepotism how can the country make progress? If the noble men of a nation punctures nationalism and its citizens deny patriotism, how can they be happy?

C. H. Zudes

Those who think little of happiness

Easily open doors to hatred

If anyone cares for his happiness

No such one will hate his neighbour

And those who hate not

Deserve no hatred

Our life is a reciprocal

All that people sow they reap.

The youth who hate others

Are missing the path of progress

If you hate to live, you love the path of death

If you neglect life, you respect death

As people who hate living, love dying.

Wounds of Love

They have taught the youth how not to forget the wounds of sordid history past, whenever they open the wounds of the days of war, when they refused to address the problems that imposed the ever dreaded war on people's destiny. Every war in human history began with hatred. Every war was simply because of avoidable ignorance, such as pride, wickedness and arrogance.

Hatred is a way of disliking things

By this some men dislike their opportunities

Why is it that many hate wars?

Still they love not nor (propose) peace

All those who hate peace

Often propagate wars

For political injustice in our countries

By this people sow the seeds of war.

For daily gossip in our homes and hamlets

C. H. Zudes

By these people neglect the mission of peace.

Gossips practice great hatred.

Those who avoid it save two lives.

Ben Sira further instructs us here;

"By hating gossip one avoids evil. He advocates, "Never repeat what you are told, and you will come to no harm. Unless it would be sinful not to, do not reveal it. Either to friend or foe do not reveal it". He says further, "You will be heard out, then mistrusted, and in due course you would be hated too".

He warns us further, "Have you heard something? Let it die with you.

Courage! It will not burst you".

Someone who talks too much will earn dislike, as someone who usurps authority will be hated". Hatred is greatest opposition to lives' progress. Hatred is a tangible branch of ignorance. And ignorance is the greatest unhealed problem in the life of men.

Wounds of Love

For if people love wisdom, they will practice it

By this, men will avoid evil and fear God

And those who fear God

These will love others.

If then people love so well

They will help the helpless.

When all in the world receives their basic help

All men will be happy.

A state of general happiness

Is a citadel of Justice

When people practice injustice, they neglect love of
wisdom and thus profess ignorance. It is a hateful sight,
to see oppression in our world. For the greatest problem
of life, requires a simple solution. Our world will be
peaceful again

C. H. Zudes

If hatred seizes to function in it for,

"Hatred has made few rich

And kept many in poverty

Yet our world is rich enough

To sustain all people in rich nature of happiness

Human world need return from its suffering

This is because of a simple problem.

That ignorance rises to control wisdom. Wisdom's refusal causes all these wars

When wisdom attempts to control ignorance, ignorance refuses and it leads men to hatred. In hatred the innocent is victimized. In hatred the prosperous often poisoned. In hatred, good leaders are assassinated. By hating, Great people die like cowards.

Examine histories...all wars began in hatred. Hatred is an of shoot of ignorance

No man values ignorance, yet majority practice it. This illicit practice has kept our world in sadness. A violent citadel of inimical events! One thing Okays hatred and

Wounds of Love

that is death, this 'Divine politics' on nature. It controls the earth.

For in death, all people regret having hated at all.

In death lovers are always happy.

For in life lovers kept on loving all things

They die happily having done all they are expected to do.

A great lover loves even death.

Such a one knows that lovers are always winners.

People who approach life with love have no regrets

Those who try to hate, always regret everything.

Better a man who hates nothing and is happy

Than those who hate someone and are sad

C. H. Zudes

Those who hate nothing can love everything.

But those who hate something can hate everything.

Hatred is ignorance let no man practice it

If people will stop hating, they have solved half of life's problems No wonder the divine instruction "Love one Another". For God gave us brain to solve all problems. And that we may give him rest. - Anon.

Why have people chosen to hate and

now their world they keep on disturbing God.

Through hatred many more problems came to exist.

Those who create problems can seldom solve any in Life.

Life is an enigmatic concept. And our world is a citadel of multiple enigmas.

When you sow the seed of love, you cultivate the practice of solution finding.

A lover of wisdom is a path finder's (philosopher), when you love more you solve your life's enigma.

Wounds of Love

Lovers have access to everything.

Haters have access to very few things.

A wise lover fears no thing

Haters fear everything including them selves

Lovers befriend everything even dangers

Acts of loving brings greatest freedom in life.

Hatred is the greatest bondage (Think well and see).

A person who hates nothing loves himself.

And those who love nothing hate even themselves.

There is no gain in hatred

And no loss in genuine love

Do not condone those who hate.

C. H. Zudes

Respect more, those who show love to all. Love is the weapon of the wise.

Hatred does more harm, and no good to users. No one who loves knowledge regrets his life. But no person who hates knowledge can be happy. A youth who hates nothing, displays ability to succeed in all things.

A student who dislikes a Teacher or his Subject, how can he understand or pass it? Hatred has a great echo of ignorance in it. Those who practice love will not delight in it. Anger hinders love and those who avoid Anger will stop hatred.

In this life, hatred is a sorrowful journey to shameful destination.

Love is a careful journey it leads to a happy destination.

The Mission of Love seems unknown to many humans! For the understanding of many people is coloured with illusions. Love is a supernatural being older than humans. A controller of humans not to be controlled by any human. Love is an enigmatic factor. The more you partake the less you possess. The lesser one partakes, the more one possesses.

Love is like an ocean

Yet it flows like a stream.

The sea of love

Are both a dungeon and a paradise

The foundation of love

Is laid in the heart of God

Love is like a diamond

Radiating from dangerous pythons

C. H. Zudes

Love is like some glittering and splendid gold

If under the earth, too deep for humans

If above the earth, too high for humans

Love shines upon earth brighter than double sunrays

Beyond the sky too high for humans

We look at love at all times

But seldom understand love!

Love studies humans, and laughs at our ignorance. Love is good yet some feel bad because of it. Love is the sweetest honey, glittering from the house of the most dangerous bee.

Love is too costly

Any cheap factor may seldom be love.

Love is a star-like, tantalizing object

Love is light radiating from deepest darkness!

Consolations of Love

Love is a universal wind meant for all people

Flowing from uncertain as it leads to uncertain end

Love is that letter

Containing no existent address.

Love is uncertainty, but uncertainty is not always love. Love is a holy business accomplishing uncertain divine task. It remains an enigma, not totally known to any! It is a glorious missionary. It has a duty of service yet an avenue of service.

Peace is a subdivision of love.

Possessing peace is a way of loving

Greater love exist in time of peace

Though human knowledge may be far

Love is more useful than man

While values of love is mightier for man

Love is a hanging friend.

C. H. Zudes

When abused by humans, it hides above their heads.

Love is an eternal treasure, though not meant for selfish possessors. It is that untouched star, seen only in the hours of darkness. Love is the only school where no one is a yet a graduate.

Love is a model of how to avoid enmity

Love helps everyone and is an enemy to no one.

In the kingdom of love

Purity and humility is the watchword.

The garments of love avoid arrogance.

Love is seated in the heavens

Those who befriend heaven cannot lose love!

Love is at home with every person

Yet many go out to seek love.

It disappears in the life of many; those who avoid conscious living cannot honour it. Love is with people

Consolations of Love

always. Those who seldom think keep searching for it. Love accepts to seem common, but when made too common fades from sight.

Love commands respect

Only respect is required to sustain love.

A non-conscious life cannot be happy

When life is not a practice of love

Love is the greatest agent of happiness

Happiness is the most important thing in life.

In the ocean of love, Man is like the swimming fish. The ocean tides of love Produces hot ocean current, People, who think less, see love as their problem.

Love is like a burden carried by woman, yet in it man is contained.

Love is an agent of justice

What anyone gives such they are bound to receive.

C. H. Zudes

Love is like a road leading to an end.

The end of the road created by love is happiness

Some fall in the road of love

By foolish action make mistakes that are self-destructive.

If you nurture love,

You will be happy in the end.

Those who water the seed of love

Are too friendly with all humans

If people manure the seed of love

Their reward is super abundant great joy.

Those who play the game of love are bound to be
careful; a watchful life is a prayer of itself. Careless
people delight in vanity and none who punctured love
had ever been happy.

Consolations of Love

When you puncture love, you devalue life. Those who destroy both, what do they possess? Be not controlled by your passion as no business is so great about loving. It is just a debt, which humans owe to fulfill. Man's love should not weaken his mission. For love's mission never stopped man possessions.

Love is equally like death

Blind is its mission towards man.

The pains of death is a vulnerable gift

When humans purchase from markets never attended.

Death is an ill answer to prayers never said

A gift granted not considering the receivers opinion.

They receive flowers that died doing good to men Some die like flower who refuse to do good to others. He is happy who think daily about a future death They are sad who never remember, death will come!

C. H. Zudes

Love is a virtue and such is love

It is meant for all to gain from

Love is a virtue

Not all are courageous to practice it.

Jealous minds will gossip more

Those who speak much expose life to danger.

There are so many gossips in this life; such has made so many problems to exist. If people gossip less, they think more. Every wise speech is a product of great thinking which is a better role than gossips.

Evil speech seems sweeter

Those who speak it take delight in wickedness.

These actions are far away from love.

Speaking too much in our world is not necessary

Consolations of Love

Where so many things are never known

Love is all embracing let none restrict it. Love is forgiveness a happy youth has no limit to the exercise of love. Do not love what is base, love is higher than such.

Prudence in loving

Will bring any youth to a happy end

God is the only central consolation of love.

TWENTY | Friendship, Love and God

Who is the standard of friendship?

He is the Omni present God

As no man is eternal

Where his love goes is eternal

Where his love came from is eternal.

He that is before all, is a friend

Love no imperfection, greater than him.

Imperfections are pictures of love.

They commit no sin

Whose love is for the sake of God?

Love that begins in God end not in men, when that begins in men, it seldom ends in God. In God love is an unclothed being in humans it is a clothed being.

C. H. Zudes

The friends that are happiest

Those whose best friend is/are their God

They Trust nothing and are seldom trusted.

They that trust not in God

"As him who trusts no one is apt to be

A man whom no one will trust" – (Anon)

A group of men do not sin, those who befriend God, a kind of action is never sin, all you do in fear of God. Each man exists in a world of solutions, who can talk to God as a friend and listening to, his answers on his daily prayers. Trust in being, is an absolute good, only when men can trust their maker.

Unwise men create love, outside God but wise men live in love, inside God.

They can never sorrow who weep only before God, they weep on who weep among men. All things are absolute where God is in charge but nothing is so certain in affairs of men.

Take time to love, it is a weapon of peace

Men who hate fall in times of war.

Friendship, Love and God

Blessings come from love

When men count none greater than God

Friendship is a bargain for curses

When men care little for the will of God

Great lovers cannot be those who hate God

For men who hate God, love no one.

I have seen that the origin of love is in God

I saw that hatred is not in the qualities of God.

Think twice and know no human love is complete. Life has taught me that God is a holistic love. This God's love is dangerous, for it, the good merit blessings, and the bad merit condemnation.

Imagine king Saul of Israel, he lost the kingdom because he did not love the God of the kingdom. So came the downfall of entire lineage. King David gained the kingdom, with a secure family blessed for eternity only because he loved God.

Better to weep, when all love is for men.

Best thing is to rejoice when greatest love is on God

C. H. Zudes

Men know not the way when they love not him

Those who fear God lack not the way.

God is a friend whose ways are less known

Yet, those who fear God share in his secrets.

If you hate God, life will be a bundle of problems

If you love God, Life is a solution.

God loves all men

But not all men love God

God is our friend

But are all, friends of God?

For "wisdom is a spirit friendly with humanity" This God is too holy, yet friendly to humans. Not all men can follow God, many are following men, and others are following things. Not all men can fear God, so many people who ought to keep the world on its feet, are ending up keeping it on its knee, as they fear and worship things that are not God.

Imagine the old people devoted to occultism they have

not taught the young that fear of God is the beginning of wisdom. But they end up dying as unwise men whose children scarcely make progress when these old one's are no more. Truly; among them are some of the very rich who are no better than animals in the forest. The rich people, who are ungodly, are not better than the king Nebuchadnezzar whom God punished to live in the forest for seven years as a beast, the royal king was feeding on grass of the forest. Yet in his majesty, affluence and wealth.

Yet not all can fear men as, they fear God

As not all men can follow men as they follow God.

Some do not know the ways of God

They are calling him, yet not praying

Men meet God every day but,

Many do not know him,

Others are visiting the house of God daily

They miss him on their ways daily

C. H. Zudes

If you do not know God

Question him and you discover him

If you know God

Be friend him, fear him and glorify him

In him alone

Can humans find perfect father and friend.

TWENTY ONE | Debts of Love

No man is happy who have no admirers

As no one is free who never admires

The mission of love is infinite

Those who avoid loving owe many debts.

Wisdom encourages love

Avoidance of love is a step of ignorance

They create enemies who consist of no love

They love always who have no enemies

It is ignorance to create enemies in life

Life is an opportunity to befriend all people.

Once love is correctly

This virtue never tarnishes.

C. H. Zudes

A wise youth feels too young for hatred, bearing in mind that life is too euphonic to deny one love. No wise one regrets a prudent love, but careless love ensnares the victims. If you must love start with God when you love be steadfast in God.

Only God is the substance of love and human love is mere imagery of his. Outside love from him, life is an illusion

A good person conquers with love

People failed as they failed to love

A life of love is a way of searching for lovers

Those who avoid love avoid life.

Life is love for those who love not live not

Those who love better live better

Love consist danger

Wisdom alone moderates the sinister in love

Careful lovers rejoice in the end

Careless lovers regret all through life

Debts of Love

Respect is greatest love in life

No love lasts, which lack respect

No one can love another

Who cannot respect another's future.

To love is the greatest virtue on earth, if you live wisely, lives problems begets joys and no sorrows. Love all people and never discriminate, such is wisdom, for greatest freedom.

If men can love you, never say no to them. If you refuse honour, shame comes your way.

Do the right thing when young

And love will be your greatest delight

If you trust in God you are trusting in love

If you trust in men, everyday is an illusion

C. H. Zudes

If you keep the right path, love is sweet

If you sin, love becomes a bitter cola.

Holiness is the greatest strength

The greatest virtue to win is love

If you are holy, its fragrance commands love

Even your enemies respect it

A holy man does not fall in love

Holiness is the model of love

If love grows weak,

Follow the path of righteousness to restore it

When you can command love, is

When you can please God

Debts of Love

Outside holiness

No man can please God

As none can please him without loving

When you cannot love

You can hardly live

Happy people do nothing without love

Lives mission is a challenge to love

Those who think rightly

These love correctly

The most correct love

Is that without sin

If you are in love and live without sin

This world will be a heaven for you

C. H. Zudes

When we meet sorrowful lovers

We discover that sin is their sorrow

Optimism makes love the best. Pessimism stains the value of love.

Rationalism makes love a king. Capitalism makes a slave of love.

Materialism destroys the spirit of love. Insincere lovers lack intelligence and

Vegetative thinkers are better than this.

The greatest lover is one

Who respects the future of the loved one

If love is without stain of sin nothing can weaken it

A wise man fears those he cannot love

He is feared by, those who cannot love him

Without love life is in prison

Pride in hatred, is pride in imprisonment

Debts of Love

Observe love and never puncture it

If you do this, problems will respect you

Do not forget to love,

Such is to forget to live

God lives for his love continues

Man dies for his love ends

If God is good then love is good, as to preach God is to preach love.

Yet not all who preach love can attempt to practice it. God is a sanctuary for all who love genuinely.

Generous loving is not, the same with genuine loving as some generous lovers fall victims of this but no genuine love is painful. If you must love let it be genuine.

The voice of love

Leads to the land of peace

C. H. Zudes

If all men could posses it

The world's problem will need no more solution

Careful love is a solution to the lover

Those who play this game lack no blessing

If it is sin to love, few men are guilty

But if it is a sin to hate, a great number commit it

So glorious it is to love, those who avoid it, loose the treasure of life.

If you hate as a youth, what will you do when old? Better then the young love that ends in happiness. No complete love is hatred on oneself. But some youth do not care, life just goes on.

Let no passion of today; destroy the mission of tomorrow for an action outside love endangers the future.

Youths' love deserve moderation

As the greatest freedom is still under law of moderacy

Debts of Love

If you must be young, beware of what you love. And if you are young, you owe the world your love.

No man is a hero, who has no love, for by loving correctly, men attain heroism.

If you think of heroes, consider what they loved. When you desire to love, imagine the life of heroes.

Heroes without love preserved no history. History is a litmus paper that qualifies love.

"I love you" is the language of youth

But I hate you no man has ever boldly said

If you care to love, you care to live

But not all who care to live cares to love

The trouble of this world, is mission without love

The peace of life is a silent mission based on love

In absence of love there is no trust

In the midst of love, trust is a culture

C. H. Zudes

When you cultivate love

    You have planted peace

If you harvest peace

    Your storehouse is ornamented with love

The path of love is not impossible

In this life, no good is impossible

Only a humble and gentle person loves peace

Love is not totally known, it is partially known to humans. The way to love seems impossible, only where and when ignorance abounds. Affection leads to love. And passion is not the best road to love, romance, is an unwise intoxicating mode of Love. Illicit sex punctures the meaning of love. If you love carelessly, you end in sin. Sin against love fertilizes future hatred.

Love is a beautiful virtue

The delightful aroma of love flow infinitely unto eternity

Men often misconceive love, but

Love both contradicts and corrects men

Debts of Love

Love is a spiritual beauty

Not destructive

If you love patiently

You will not be corrupt

Blessed are they who love wisely and they live long

Some still hate, these die early

Love is a culture, a gift and language of God.

C. H. Zudes

TWENTY TWO | Love and Prayer

Those who pray love the master key of all problems' solutions. Not all who love prayer can practice it with love. Some love prayers but still pray without love.

Not all who dislike prayer can hate their neighbour. Though many hate others and possessing many enemies, yet these pretend to love prayer. Some are prayerful but do not pray.   A man who prays well   is aware of the presence of the divine.

What then is prayer?

"It is awareness, awareness, and awareness"

A conscious life is a praying life.

Those who are never conscious, seldom pray.

Power of consciousness

Is the strength of observation.

C. H. Zudes

This leads to ability and power to overcome!

By praying awareness is created of the presence of God

Prayer raises man in communion with God. When a prayerful person falls. The love of prayers may preserve him. Prayer is the seed of religion. A certain religion exist but do not yet pray.

The truth is that everything seems to be prayer, yet there is time for prayers

Those who love it, pray consciously. Those who dislike it, equally pray but unconsciously.

But which prayer is actually heard?

Which does God answer?

"To live a life without prayer is like

Growing a Garden full of weeds"- Anon.

As confusions are more

When people pray less

Love and Prayer

Trials decrease when

Humans increase prayer.

"To train a child without religion

Is to make his a clever devil" –Anon.

Therefore religion's seed

Weakens the weapons of human destruction!

Why do some tell inimical story of blessed mornings?
Why seem qualified to begin a day without prayer? Mid
night may be time for clash of powers

Does wisdom qualify a man to sleep without praying?

'I do not know how to pray!'

How then do you learn how to eat?

In deed those who pray more eat less

As those who eat less, pray more!

C. H. Zudes

Prayer is a hope for happy end. But when prayer constitutes an unhappy end!

Was that prayer answered? Can prayer ever be harmful to humans?

Prayer is spiritual a ceaseless phenomenon! Human life is neither certain nor everlasting!

Prayer and life, which is more necessary?

Life and prayer, which is a superior being?

Is it then better to live long and never pray?

Or to pray well for brief existence?

Is every lover of prayer living happily?

Or are all unhappy people those who never pray well?

An actual friend proves

How life is a prayer

A certain kind of friend does not pray, but admires those whose prayer is a life force. If prayer is done properly, it becomes a necessity to follow up, works and reason. Awareness through prayer is a gradual movement in the road to success.

The Zenith of universal love is a consistent selfless prayer life. To attain happiness is not so difficult yet this can never be done without prayer.

Some pray through thinking

Yet many pray through wishing.

The best kind of prayer is

That prompted by awareness.

Those who avoid conscious existence

Simply avoid prayers

By living consciously, wise ones avoid sin

By habit of holiness, people live prayerful lives.

C. H. Zudes

TWENTY THREE | Love and Happiness

A conscious life is a happy one; a watchful life in existence is smooth and joyful. A humble mind is always aware of its humility. It is by this that virtue endures, outside awareness a man contradicts himself.

No man is happy when life becomes a contradiction of purpose.

Any who claims happiness

May hardly be sincere

A man who is sincere, needs

Consciousness to preserve it

Happiness is the end aim of everything

Those who attain it had it in mind

Success outside happiness

Is like an Iroko tree without roots

No giant is himself if he is not powerful

C. H. Zudes

So is an end in view not aiming at happiness

Those who contradict virtues fade soon in history

Those who drink much are victims of intoxication

So is every careful program leading to a happy end n   o value is better than happiness. For all we call good intends to produce it.

If you are not happy do not pretend

Pretence over this does not lead to it

People who never think well before an action

Seldom calculate their end

An unhappy end in life

Has made many ought to be heroes, pretenders

Those who aim, to become heroes

Always have purpose for a happy end

A comic hero is popular at least for a happy end. Comic nature of heroes Implies they ended happily and truly than tragic sorrow of anti heroes or ...

Love and Happiness

If you are never happy stop worrying, one truth is necessary that, a planned life is your solution.

Are you not aware of how to become happy?

Simply be aware of things to do and things to avoid

Happiness is your goal

Only to those who have goals in life

An unhappy thing is an unplanned one

A tragic hero

Have got much but lost a happy end

If you end unhappily, try again

But let awareness become your watchword

I am not happy, is a statement

Of those who planned not and began

If you lost happiness you have lost a goal

If you gained it, you have gained some gold

A selfish leader can never be happy

C. H. Zudes

Selfishness is a vice and ruins its possessor

A selfish person often knows not

For such an action is often unconscious

Emotional minds yearn for selfishness

None of these is an intelligible foundation.

Only an intelligent man

Can readily become happy

Those who blame others

Prove how unhappy they have become

Any happy person is calm

When wronged they give only corrections

If you cannot correct, learn to avoid blames

Blames have done no good in history. Blames have led into wars and non-ended happily. An interior mind forgets the game of blame. A busy mind, is condition for a happy future.

Love and Happiness

If you chose to be happy

Chose also to avoid evil

For evil is readily a deprivation

All vices hinders the way to happiness

Only happiness is worth having

Therefore, let us all avoid sin!

Those who gossip keep on sinning

These foil the stable life of others

It is to their woe that they can use their mouth

But cannot make the world a happier place

Happiness is something natural and certain

In the two places where life is worth living

Life on earth aims at happiness

Those in heaven need no option

C. H. Zudes

A blessed journey is a successful one

A successful person counts his blessings

This entire groups needs one thing that, is happiness

Everybody has one aim in life

Every struggle is an attempt to end happily

An interior mind forgets the game of blames

A busy mind, is condition for a happy future

If you chose to be happy

Chose also to avoid evil

For evil is readily a deprivation

All vices hinders the way to happiness

Only happiness is worth having

Therefore, let us all avoid sin!

Love and Happiness

Those who gossip keep on sinning

 These foil the stable peace of the world

It is sad they have strength

But cannot make the world a happier place

Disordered love of a man, denies the man Happiness. Life of happiness is all humanity seeks. The only route to it is, fulfill your own duty. A blessed journey is a successful one. A successful person counts his blessings. This entire group needs one thing that is happiness.

Everybody has one aim in life

This one single desire further equals humanity.

Both the rich thinks of having it

The poor is consoled by it

Better a happy poor man

Than an angry rich man

Not all the rich can find the rest of mind

C. H. Zudes

If you neglect the happy way you gain worry

If you have not become rich

Take shelter in happiness, it is a treasure

Many rich people are seeking this

And have preferred to become poor

A generous life is a happy one

A kind giver plans for future happiness

This group makes others happy

In truth no one can give what he lacks

If you play the game of politics and win

Look after the poor and be holy

There is an assignment God has given you, do all you can to carry, to carry it out. If you neglect this, street beggars are better than you. At least, some beggar's are happier than some of the rich.

That nothing is a problem

Is the truth to learn about life

    All we see as problems

Are necessary conditions for a reason

Everything is an opportunity

Whether good or bad

Do not regret that you are suffering

For only when it is over, you will rejoice.

A kind of suffering is inevitable; a second kind is educational challenge.

If you do well in your youth, how can you be a beggar in your old age? If you refuse to do well in your youth, who will be blamed if you end up a beggar?

The historic tale between the rich man and Lazarus is a unique chapter to contemplate on. As the rich man had every pleasure he wanted to enjoy, but with this he created an avoidable problem because of ignorance and selfishness. Yet, Lazarus, the one who naturally could be seen as having poverty as his problem, traded his difficulty positively to win favour for himself in heaven. Today his name is even heroic and noble people answer it. But the rich man ended in shame that neither history nor humans are proud of him today, even when he had everything he needed. He enjoyed today and suffered tomorrow.

The truth is all men are bound to suffer.

See then suffering, as road to success.

When you fail to suffer in your youth

You are bound to suffer more in your old age.

Those, you failed to conquer in youth's time

Will return to you in your old age

Those who spend time to complain are creating

Non-existent problems into the world

Fear one alone you can solve all your problems.

If you discuss your problems with God,

Jubilee Harvest of Problems and Solutions

Then tell me how that problem can have no solution, if you can readily do the right thing, then you will discover how all things are opportunities for heroic events.

If love be your watch word

How can you not solve everything?

If another refuses to love all things

How can things agree to be solved by him?

Those who solve problems are not the arrogant type

Those who are not wicked easily triumph

Yet all problems have necessity to exist.

They exist for some unknown pragmatic necessity.

If problems are what we make of them! How is the light not needed in the morning, the greatest need of the night? How can the food not needed to the well-fed person, be the only savior in the hand for the hungry person? If you know this well, you will have no problem in this life.

Our world is a home not only of problems

C. H. Zudes

But also of solutions

But some people think out illusions

Who think more, only of problems

Never let yourself create problems you cannot solve.

Thus you will become one of the happiest humans.

If any creature falls into problem,

Just be patient and work hard

If mine can be solved, yours can also be solved.

If human problem is ignorance

Who then is ignorant?

Ignorance! It bows to proper knowledge

All problems bow to men alike!

As in the views of Heraclitus the Philosopher, "out of what differs, comes the most beautiful harmony", so is your present difficulty a means of harmony for happiness in the near but unknown future! If not, why are student's attempt and stressing at studies today, an authority for them after school?

Jubilee Harvest of Problems and Solutions

Why is a merchant's labour in the market or at sea, the strength of his riches?

Problems are equally friendly with men

That is why they keep coming.

> Humans are the bee

> Problems are the honey

Step beyond the physical and

Discover that God is readily

Waiting to solve all problems

If people refuse to think they have refused to solve

What they call their problems.

Men need to be happy in this life

But some fear much their challenging problems

Such seldom think out solutions.

Yet no problem is too hard for a friend.

That it cannot be penetrated and solved.

C. H. Zudes

If you solve many problems do not be over Joyful

For you simply fulfilled a cultural mission of life.

If you cannot solve problems do not relent

For the mission of your creation is still un-fulfilled

Those who carefully solve problems are

Like students who pass examinations of life

Man has no reason to fear his problems

    Even at death, a mission is ending

    and another starting.

All that humans need to do is to plan life

But no wise planning will exclude God.

If you depend wisely on God

Tell me what you cannot do well

Jubilee Harvest of Problems and Solutions

When you befriend your problems,

Friendship becomes the key that unlocks doors.

It will unlock all life's difficulties.

This life is not a burden of problems to carry.

It is a game, a business of how you negotiated

It successfully, negotiate all fine, get all in stages

Of life to your advantage!

TWENTY FIVE | Epilogue Sonnet Poems

| MOTHER AFRICA |

Thou seem now, poorest of all continents

Not because thou art un-endowed with riches.

Children in thee! Ignorant of thy possession

In little knowledge, they waste thy resources.

Children seldom partake in thy resources.

Poor reasoning controlled by bullets

People still sorrow because of hunger, others amulets

But who art these bulging stomachs, the land inhabits?

Human erosion, eroding thy resources

Glorious potentials fly to other continents

While powerful weakness with thee remains!

Why Black Leader? Black Leader Why?

C. H. Zudes

"Who is still molesting children of thy Birth?

Empower thy people, develop their father land

War an evil culture, what good art thou to Africans?

Black hair think, oh black hair think!

Epilogue Sonnet Poems

|YOUTH of AFRICA|

Thou art little humans sprouting

Thou art human shrub nature inhabits.

Little beings honour to thy growth

Calm down! Fortune surrounds thee!

Family setting enshrines thee!

Fear less, just be obedient

Count well, thy seeds to sow

Cool down, heavy thy harvest!

Evil in history never inherit.

Think well as none's slave to become

Be thou the correct seeds of time

Correct the weakness of history, past

Oh Youth, count-less, images that-fade

Oh Youth pay debts thou owe in knowledge

C. H. Zudes

Oh Youth thy gone forget, thy future prepare!

Teach the world thou came to birth...

Like Michael Angelo speak with talent to
paint the new idea

Like Florence Nightingale be the song, the
voice of talent

Like Michael Jackson employ the world to for
thy music

With the song that Africa can change, in your
hand and time

Epilogue Sonnet Poems

| IRONY OF JUSTICE |

When men perverts Justice

Evil seeds from among them sprout

Goodness hidden, evil erupts

Sorrow hidden in the heart of all

Happiness enemy to all involved!

Shame embraces the wise!

Delight in evil for the wise!

The seed of injustice of men!

Joy fades in the life of men!

When men nurture injustice

They weep to harvest their future

Conflict never to fade among them

Lovers of evil, ever to regret!

They depart from the laws of the most high!

C. H. Zudes

| NIGERIA MY COUNTRY! |

By thy name image of Black Africans

Multi speech, people and culture

Art these meant for enmity and wars?

How many things hast thou invented?

But patriotism sinks in the hand of Nepotism

But tribalism cracks the egg-yolk of Nationalism

Stranger's capitalism devalue strength of African
Pragmatism

Oh Black leader, Black Leader, Black leaders arise!

Art thou known for "wetting" Nigeria?

What a slow pace of civilization!

Who bewitches thy children's Education?

Art thou not rich, who stole thy wealth?

Who punctures this tube of justice?

Epilogue Sonnet Poems

Arrogant sons who claim to be prominent!

Who are these, a set of leaders?

Ah! Who shed these pools of blood?

Who brought on thee these coups?

Giant! Recover! From brutish mentality

Strengthen thy fellows!

Children of Africa stare at thee!

C. H. Zudes

| NGWO: MY HOME TOWN: |

Thou blest, simple but mighty

Peopled, of gentle heroes

Centre of eastern lands, home of coal

Popular nodal town unites the nation!

Sprouting silent giants but prominent figures

Peace lovers, not always fight on lands

Little wickedness consists in thee

Idle people seldom in thee

What professors

What inventors hast thou produced?

Prepare more, prominent people from thee to arise

Few heroes are never sufficient

Land of precious subversive stream in West Africa

Epilogue Sonnet Poems

Soap suds enters thy children's eye

Art thou honoured by Coal

that flammable Stone

Lacking neither civility,

nor art thou well developed?

Thou a debt to give peace a chance!

Put away any sympathy to culture

So goodness may from thee sprout!

PHANTOM HOUSE

EPILOGUE

This book is a nonfiction, a letter from the author to everyone of this generation, friends, both the younger and the elderly. This is because, the young people of a generation are the most precious jewels and ornament that any society is capable of being proud of, economically, socially and even politically they are the best assets, but in black-hairs society like ours, they are often understood as liabilities in this business of investing in a life time.

A healthy example can be seen in this contemporary and logical truth.

Imagine the situation where many young unemployed people have now laboured to develop their talents, ready to help rebuild their society, but no one funds them, they can employ other tender upcoming job seekers, but they have no means to pay salaries, at the same time only about 3 percent of the entire citizenry have almost pocketed the wealth of the nation, the resources of the continent and we are calm in the face of these evil fires burning. But are they busy playing the ostrich, in that local rich-men mentality? Are our political leaders to be called rich-men or heroes of a defeated camp?

Keeping to their own wasteful-un-usefulness, about 95 percent of the money meant for the entire national economy, depositing their excess reserve in banks of most developed economies. In the face of these irascible actions, the government of nations are silent, pretending to be handicapped to change this evil situation inherited. What then is government, if you cannot bring great positive changes to an inherited brutish society's immoral mechanism? But if the spirit of pragmatism is allowed to influence our age and time, the youth will be practically involved in changing the world for good.

In the spiritual and psychoanalysis of age and time, you discover that there is a disconnect in moral order of human society. The young Girls consider a life of holiness and remaining virgins as things of the past, the young men consider holiness and acts of becoming saints and moral leaders of society as obsolete. 'Religion' has almost destroyed spirituality!

Professional prostitution is a stinking culture now, but even the apparent elderly people in society, politicians have turned eyes-right, when the moral life of the young people which defines the eugenics of the future generation is thrown in the mud, into this dust-bin of human history. Many young women now count in tens, the number of "Abortions" they have done, before they arrive at the stage of settling down for marriage. Is this now an African culture?

Youthhood in Africa

Going on in this moral crisis, the western world projects the immoral acts and senseless evil of human-animalism in these theories of Gay marriages, Homo-sexuality, Lesbianism and Sodomy etc. Where then is the African morality?

Did the elders uphold not this? Thus the youth of Africa faces this dilemma of, rhetorically asking through their daily actions, in vibrant soliloquy; in endless monologue; which one exactly is better? Is it the western immorality or the African morality?

My few words for the youth are; never emulate evil from anyone; observe that no great person, inventor or scientist in all aspects of human history, is an immoral person. These evils take away human intelligence. The Holy Spirit of wisdom and instruction departs from every such act that offends God Z. As a result, no evil actions today will bring solution or answers to the questions that the challenges in life, will ask to your desired great future, so avoid evil and fear God.

Surely, if you do, all things in life will end well for you.

Do not follow the ways of the wicked for the days of the wicked are very short. "Soon when you look around, the wicked will be nowhere to be found, with no name left behind" says the Lord, the Almighty God. The road of the righteous is bright and brighter than the sun. Have nothing to do with lies and misleading life. Avoid evil

Z1. You will be prosperous, if you read the word of God from beginning to the end daily to practice it Z2. Evil done today, will crumble the root of greatness tomorrow, so do not copy evil ways.

Do not abandon God, take wisdom serious, and nothing in life will stand on your way or make you stumble. When the earth-quake that brings crisis to human life come your way, only the healthy spirituality and relationship with God will sustain you. Consider King David and King Hezekiah Z3 when they fell into difficulty, they recovered only because each of them, told God to remember the covenant they made with him in their youth. What will you remind God of about your youth days?

When crisis of life bring with it confusions, only your friendship with God brings you direction.

Everything in life can happen to you. But the greatest wisdom I have seen in life is in these words that; "Greatness lies in adversity" z4 as you will learn in the views of Mozart Amadeus Wolfang, the Genius of classical music.

Beyond all these, in this life, there is something called interior Locutio.Z5

Mr James Chukwuemeka Ozoude

Mr James Chukwuemeka Ozoude (Ultimate Electronics)

Nine years with the Ancestors, the long journey you began at the apex of your youth leaving a vacuum in our lives no one else can fill. Rest In Perfect Peace.

The Author: Left, With Bishop Michael Eneja of Blessed Memory. Also, is Mr. Agustine Odinikpo during the 1997 Apostolic Year/Work: Right

Parting picture at end of graduation exams 2004 of Young
Philosophers of Nnamdi Azikiwe Universtiy, Awka, Nigeria.

Middle: The H.O.D Rev. Fr. Dr. Bona Christus Umogu and Prof. Ike H.
Odimuegwu To the extreme Left: the Author, Chris Ozoude, President
of the Student's Association.

GLOSSARY

Aboki |

An Hausa, Nigerian title for a young man who is not yet a Mallam or a mister. It often used in synonym to 'friend'.

I no dey |

There is none of it, or is not there

REFERENCES

Chapter 1

A   As in Joseph Omoregbe`s book on contemporary
ETHICS: SYSTEMATIC AND HISTORIC STUDY.

B   Gen. Ikemba Emeka Ojukwu on Ahiara declaration, a
Promulgation during the Biafra and Nigeria 3 years war.

C   Ideas of Philip D. Curtin in his book IMAGE OF
AFRICA

D   Basil Davidson in his book: THE ANCIENT PAST

D1   Ecclesiastics   (Sirach 25: 2).

Chapter2

1.D2   Key note address of Former Vice Chancellor
Professor Pita Ejiofor during the Send forth of 2002
graduating students of Nnamdi Azikiwe

University, Awka Eastern Nigeria.

Chapter 3

E   (Proverb 22:6).

Chapter 4.

F   (Psalm 72:7).

G   (Psalm.111: 10).

Chapter 5

H   The written remark of Bishop Desmond TUTU,

(1978:356)

I   Ecclesiastics (Sirach 42:8).

J   (Matthew 19:13-15).

Chapter 6

K   How Europe Underdeveloped Africa by Walter Rodney

L   Word of T.T Munger

M   German word for 'Just being there' doing no thing

N   Tigritude is a theory in the study of African Philosophy

Chapter 7

O   Sunday Sun News of June 3, 2012 page 4.

P   (Gani Fawehimi in an interview on television point Blank 29 Dec 2000).

Chapter 8

Q   (psalm 119 –9).

Chapter 9

R   (2 Thess. 2: 3, 4-12).

S   Thomas Merton on Breeding of Churches pg 21-34

T   Job 15-25.

U   (Apostolicam A. 3,12)

V   Ecclesiastics (Sirach ch.46-48)

About the Author

Chris-Tony Ozoude-chi has a Bachelor (Hon.) degree in the Science of Philosophy, was president of the campus arm of the National Association of Philosophy Students, Nnamdi Azikiwe University Awka, and Prefect of St. John Cross Seminary Nsukka. Chris is determined to exalt the ethics of pragmatic philosophy for healthy nation building. He is charitable and enjoys to see the wise stand up for their rights and bring healing to the problems of nations making this world a better place. To Chris, NOTHING GOOD IS IMPOSSIBLE UNDER THE SUN.

Youthhood in Africa is the author's second novel. For more books by Chris Ozoude, visit our website or request our books at your local retail bookstore.

www.ingramcontent.com/pod-product-compliance
Lightning Source LLC
LaVergne TN
LVHW091246080426
835510LV00007B/142